Vocational Education and Guidance:
A System for the Seventies

Vocational Education and Guidance: A System for the Seventies

James A. Rhodes
Governor of the State of Ohio

Charles E. Merrill Publishing Company
A Bell & Howell Company
Columbus, Ohio

International Standard Book Number: 0-675-09265-5

Library of Congress Catalog Card Number: 72-135887

1 2 3 4 5 6 7 8—75 74 73 72 71 70

Printed in the United States of America

PREFACE

In many ways the success of our nation in its social, political and economic functions has been due to our American system of free public education. This system, which served us well in the earlier years of our development, simply has not kept pace with the increased responsibilities that must be accepted in a technological world in which the contribution of each person both socially and economically is important.

Our system of public education grew to maturity in the period of time in which most of us could receive information about jobs from the work of our parents and on the job training in industry, or employment in unskilled occupations.

The emphasis in the early years of our educational system has been on basic literacy training for most youth and college preparation for a few. This system which has failed to adjust to a modern day, as outlined in my book, Alternative to a Decadent Society, represents the only true resource for the development of solutions to our social and economic problems. Within this book I propose a system of vocational guidance and vocational education to be established at the core of the curriculum starting with the kindergarten which can serve as a means of changing the direction of the massive public education system in this nation without attempting to duplicate that system.

It proposes a system to prepare youth for choice in training of his plan for employment and a concept for implementing that choice through vocational, technical or professional preparation.

I would express appreciation to the State Department of Education of Ohio for material provided for parts of the book with particular appreciation to the Division of Vocational Education and Division of Guidance and Testing for assistance received from these units.

James A. Rhodes

CONTENTS

vii

Chapter 1   THE EDUCATION-
EMPLOYMENT MISMATCH

A Critical Problem

Society, like Nature, abhors a vacuum. Just as Nature often fills a vacant lot with weeds, so Society often fills a newly-created need with inadequate services. Until a nation can develop more realistic solutions, inadequate social services are tolerated. As long as the need for a change in a social service is not critical to society, it is allowed to continue in its original form, without drastic alteration.

To paraphrase Abraham Lincoln, "Our nation is now involved in a great battle to determine if that nation, or any nation so conceived and dedicated, can maintain a technological and affluent society in which many of the traditional family relationships and social institutions no longer match the demands of that society." The industrial revolution and technical evolution have demanded that our social institutions perform services formerly provided by the family and the work pattern of the people.

Two of the forces contributing to the greatness of America have been the Judeo-Christian work ethic and our system of public

1

education, which has provided a literate populace. The future of our nation rests partly with the continuation of the Judeo-Christian work ethic, and the provision of jobs to enable all able-bodied citizens to practice that ethic. Our nation's future also will depend upon a massive change in our public education system. We need to recognize the greater responsibilities that must be placed upon that system due to changes in our total way of life, including our family life, which bring about the need for further changes unprecedented in the history of man.

There is no way to maintain our way of life or to eliminate poverty except by the contribution of all able-bodied people to the economy through meaningful and productive work. Increasing technology will not permit people to enjoy a life of ease and luxury without accompanying hard work. While the number of workers required for manufacture of goods may decrease as a percentage of the work force, there is an insatiable demand for services which can utilize the abilities and skills of all the people.

With all of the great possibilities ahead of us as a nation, we find ourselves in the midst of a growing demand for educational services which our educational system is unprepared, unable, or unwilling to provide. In this book I will direct attention to only one of the new responsibilities placed upon the educational system as a result of our technological age, but changes to accept that responsibility may be at the core of the total change that must be brought about if our public education system is to continue to serve our social order effectively.

In the days of Abraham Lincoln children learned many things from home experiences which are denied to modern youth. The young men and women of Lincoln's day were not brought into the world by families who could afford to treat them as luxuries, or as alter-egos. They quickly found that they were an integral part of a family unit in which all parts of that unit had to contribute through work in order for the family to survive. The work was not "made work" for which they received an allowance far beyond the contribution to the family, but was real work in which the participation of the individual in that work gave them a sense of belonging. Many of the young people observed their fathers and mothers at work and quite often gained the skills and knowledge necessary for either their life's work or for their first job by working along with them. The educational system served relatively simple functions of developing a literate nation in terms of reading, writing, and arithmetic, and providing a basic understanding of our republican form of government. Schools also served the function of bringing together people from the various walks of life—except for the most affluent persons who then, as today, could utilize private schools for the education of their youth.

Today it is impossible for most young people to observe their father at work, much less to learn the skills necessary for entrance into employment by working with their father. The two-wage-earner family, where the father and mother are both working, has made it difficult for the girls to learn budgeting, homemaking and child care from the mother at home. At a time in which the preparation for a first job is of greater importance than ever before, we find that it is impossible for most boys and girls to gain the necessary skills and technical knowledge for entrance into modern employment through family relationships.

Little was demanded of the public school system during the early days of its organization regarding the preparation of people for work. Hence as education expanded into the upper elementary school and high school levels the system considered only the needs of those who planned to go on to preparation for a vocation at the college level. We are faced in a technological age with an education system that is at least one hundred years out of date. The antiquated curricula stress a study of disciplines in a manner which is not based in either educational theory or educational psychology and assumes that the study of isolated disciplines is the means of preparing for life as well as for college.

Research does not prove that this subject-centered approach prepares students either for life or for college. An analysis of selected studies between 1923 and 1964 by Dr. Collins W. Burnett, professor of higher education at the Ohio State University, showed:

1. If this group of studies is representative of the research that has been done by this area, it seems possible that college has placed too much emphasis on a specific pattern of high school units for college admission.

2. Better research designs need to be constructed to test this problem. Perhaps the individual college should enter into a cooperative arrangement with the high schools from which it receives large numbers of graduates.

3. High school counselors may be in position to counsel high school students in terms of which courses will meet their educational goals with less emphasis on what the students need to succeed in college.

4. Academic success in college may be a function of individual intelligence, motivation, value pattern and work skills rather than completion of a certain number of units in subject matter fields.[1]

One study reported was by Paul B. Diedrich, in which Mr. Diedrich stated,

> The only requirement for entrance into the University of Chicago . . . is that students be able to read, write and think a good deal better than most students are now able to do. . . . simple tests of these three abilities have a higher correlation with marks in all courses than any other measure it has ever devised . . .

> Our system of public secondary schools, therefore, is in the grip of a standard curriculum which is based on the fundamental premise that the pursuit of certain prescribed studies is essential to success in college. It has been proved, as completely as anything in life is ever proved, that this premise is false.[2]

Such studies, and the growing tendency of universities to accept students on the basis of examination rather than Carnegie units earned in high school, make us ask whether our antiquated curriculum is caused by our universities or by the attitudes of

---

[1] Collins W. Burnett, "Studies Dealing with the Relationship between a Prescribed Pattern of High School Units for Entrance Requirements and Academic Success in College," Enclosure with *Ohio Guidance News and Views* (Ohio State Department of Education, Division of Guidance and Testing), September/October, 1967.

[2] *Ibid.*

teachers and administrators in our public schools who have developed great resistance to change. Our system of public education seems to reflect the concept, "After all, this is the way we have always done it, and this is the way the parents of the children expect us to teach." Most teachers and administrators are the product of the school system which they now direct. They successfully jumped the educational hurdles in that system, moved to the college level, where they successfully jumped additional academic hurdles, and are now directing a school system in which they assume if they just make the subjects harder the needs of students and society will be met.

The reluctance of school administrators to radically change the educational system, however, may not be so much a problem of administrator and teacher attitudes as changing parental attitudes when those attitudes often determine whether funds will be made available to continue the educational programs. Too many parents who were not successful in the present antiquated curriculum, or were less successful than the top students, want to measure their children in relationship to the top students of their memory by having them jump the same hurdles. They remember that the top students took certain subjects and often watched those top students go on to professional careers. They want to compete again through their own young people, and make the mistake of thinking that the educational curriculum of thirty or forty years ago is an adequate curriculum for today.

This attitude of the parents carries over to the student body. We find most high schools controlled by a small group of intellectually able students who can jump all the necessary academic hurdles, regardless of whether those hurdles have meaning for them or not, and thus the vast majority of students infer that they are second-class or inferior, particularly if they dare to participate in job-training through a vocational program at the high-school level. The blunt facts in Ohio are shown by Figure 1-1.

We live in a snobbish society. As John Gardner, former Secretary of Health, Education, and Welfare, stated, "We live in a society which honors poor philosophy, because philosophy is an honorable calling, and ignores good plumbing, because plumbing is a humble occupation. Under such practices, we will have neither

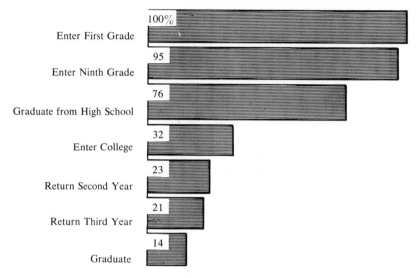

Enter First Grade	100%
Enter Ninth Grade	95
Graduate from High School	76
Enter College	32
Return Second Year	23
Return Third Year	21
Graduate	14

Source: Ohio State Dept. of Education, School Year 1965-66.

FIGURE 1-1

OHIO'S EDUCATIONAL PROGRAM

good philosophy, nor good plumbing. Neither our pipes nor our theories will hold water."

Over the years, the pontifical attitudes of top representatives from industry have helped to maintain our antiquated system of education by applauding the emphasis upon the education of the intellectually elite through the system of hard academic subjects. Too often the industrialist has told the school what he thought they wanted to hear, "Just give me the well-rounded individual, and I'll do the rest." At the hiring gate, however, the person responsible for the work in the factory or in the business has to ask, "What can you do?" And young people attempting to enter the work force too often have to answer, "I am willing to do anything." Ohio's State Superintendent of Public Instruction, Dr. Martin Essex, has pointed up that for the first time in the history of man, a man's strength—a strong back—cannot guarantee him a living. Most expanding industries and businesses of today no longer talk about the well-rounded individual, but look to the availability of trained manpower, or of sources for training manpower.

For years Ohio has led the nation in industrial growth and we know that industries, relocating or expanding, look to the availability of vocational education programming as a source for services for new employees and upgrading of existing employees. Industries and businesses do not attempt to impose their desires upon the education system and over the years they consistently have been supporters of our educational program. They cannot continue, however, to operate highly technical industries with the unskilled and untrained youth who are dropouts of our high schools and colleges or the graduates from the general course in our public schools.

An institution which refuses to recognize the basic problem of our society is outdated and threatened. Our education system is outdated, yet it is this very system which holds our only hope for the future. The educational system flatly neglects up to 70 percent of the young people in school. In doing so, it creates dropouts, delinquents, unemployables and welfare recipients. The system does not accept the social problem from a practicable point of view and has refused to be responsible for the job preparation of youth of America. If our society denies youth the opportunity to learn about work through the home, or through the work of the father, and if the home no longer can accept the responsibility for preparing youth for initial employment, then our educational system must accept this responsibility.

Need for Improved Guidance and Vocational Education in the Public Schools

For the first time in the recorded history of man, the number of unskilled workers in the work force represents a declining segment of the population. Most jobs, including most of the semi-skilled occupations, will require preparation in terms of skills and technical knowledge for a successful entrance into that occupation. The jobs in the technological age will demand basic background and education in terms of reading and numerical skills. In addition they will require a study of the application of math and science to the occupational area for which they are prepared to enable them to adjust to changes in their occupations or to learn new occupations as our technological age increases its pace, thus changing our work patterns.

We find ourselves in an economy in which the most physically able segment of our population (ages 18 to 24) has an unemployment rate three times that of the normal population. Looking at some facts about one state which show how the system of education treats the problem of occupational preparation, we find that in this state the members of the work force distribute themselves as:

	1960*	1975**
Craftsmen, foremen and kindred workers	16%	16%
Skilled operators and kindred workers	22	21
Service workers	11	12
Unskilled workers	5	2
Agriculture		
Managers & operators	3	2
Farm laborers	1	0
Sales workers	8	9
Clerical and kindred workers	15	16
Manager and proprietors	8	8
Professional and technical workers	11	14

* 1960 Census data for Ohio
** Projection data of the Ohio State Employment Service

Now if we would review how we prepare our high school youth for the world of work, we would discover the curriculum enrollment figures to be as shown by Figure 1-2. The job market in the State of Ohio and in the nation is changing. There are fewer jobs available for unskilled workers, and farm labor is disappearing. There are growing opportunities for employment in service, clerical, technical and professional job areas. All of these jobs, however, require education: vocational, technical and professional. It is obvious that if our schools are to expand services in vocational, technical and professional education, such programs can be effective only if there is an effective program or system of guidance to serve all youth. Several years ago Dr. Leon Lesinger, then a superintendent of schools in San Mateo, Cali-

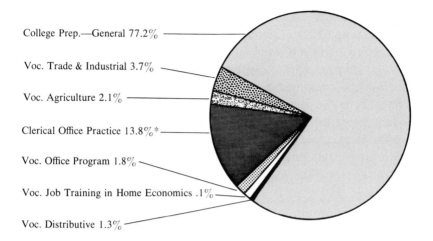

College Prep.—General 77.2%

Voc. Trade & Industrial 3.7%

Voc. Agriculture 2.1%

Clerical Office Practice 13.8%*

Voc. Office Program 1.8%

Voc. Job Training in Home Economics .1%

Voc. Distributive 1.3%

Source: Ohio State Dept. of Education, Grades 11 and 12, 1965-66.
* This figure includes students enrolled for personal use and exploration.
Not all have vocational intent or achieve the necessary skills.

FIGURE 1–2

HIGH SCHOOL ENROLLMENT BY
GAINFUL OCCUPATIONAL PROGRAMS

fornia, predicted the growth of student unrest at the high-school level; he placed the blame upon the lack of relevance of the educational program in which the youth were enrolled. We have continued to ignore the fact that completion of a high school education is expected of all youth, not just the intellectual elite, who alone completed high school as late as thirty years ago. In 1955, for example, only 55 percent of the youth starting the first grade in Ohio were completing high school. This percentage has now grown to 76 percent for the State of Ohio as a whole, but in the inner sections of our major cities, the dropout rate often still reaches the 50 percent figure.

Our educational system must be for all youth. It must provide success experiences. It must enable graduates to enter and compete in a modern technological society. Students are rebelling, and no wonder. At both the high-school and college levels they are questioning a curriculum which assists and rewards only those students who, because of their intellectual capacity, will tend to "make it" anyway. In 1969 Dr. Bruno Bettelheim, professor of psychiatry at the University of Chicago, gave some interesting testimony to a special sub-committee on education of the House of Representatives. Dr. Bettelheim stated that the most rebellious students, here and abroad, are students of the social sciences and humanities; few are in the professional colleges of medicine, engineering and natural sciences because they are "busy doing things that are important to them." Dr. Bettelheim's main point was that many students are perplexed. He stated:

> It is those students who do not quite know what they are preparing themselves for and why, the students who sit around waiting for examinations, rather than doing active work—who form the cadres of student rebellion. In my opinion, there are today far too many students in the colleges who essentially have no business to be there. Some are there to evade the draft, many others have a vague idea that it will help them to find better-paying jobs, though they do not know what jobs they want, and again many go to college because they do not know what better to do and because it is expected of them. Their deep dissatisfaction with themselves and their inner confusion is projected against the institution of the university first, and against all institutions of society secondarily, which are blamed for their own inner weaknesses.

Dr. Bettelheim argued that many of the young men in college today "would be better off in a high level program of vocational education which is closely linked to a work program, which gives scope to their needs for physical activity, and visible, tangible achievement."

The statements made by Dr. Bettelheim in relationship to the students at the university undoubtedly have implications for students enrolled in our public schools. Youth are confused. They are told not to worry about preparing for work until they are old enough. They are told too often that the only honorable jobs are those in the professions. They are told that the real educational program is the "college preparatory curriculum," in which only a small percentage of the students can achieve. Then upon graduation from high school, or upon dropping out from college they receive the admonition, "Go to work," when they have nothing to sell a technological age but a strong back, and that technological age isn't buying a strong back. They have been taught by school teachers who have a safe career that the only way of life is to prepare for such a safe career. Most of them will not have a career of a stable nature, but may have a series of vocations, occupations, or just jobs. Too many youth are bewildered, afraid, unready and unwilling to cope with such a dilemma. A short period of time with a guidance counselor, looking over job information sheets, provides no answers to the young person preparing to enter a hard and impersonal world which continually asks, "What can you do?" Undoubtedly, this massive problem, which has not been faced by any previous generation in the same degree as this generation, has a greater influence on youth to "cop out" than some of the idealism given as the reason. The idealism is real but the same idealism was present in the youth of many previous generations. The problem is the opportunity for the youth to interject himself into our society in such a manner that he can realize a self-identity and feel a relationship to social action for the improvement of mankind.

The vocational guidance program in the public school has been a failure. It has not provided youth with the understanding of the economic society in which they find themselves, nor encouraged them to follow an educational program which would enable them to compete in such a society. The guidance impact of the total educational system, starting with kindergarten, completely overwhelms any minor contact the student may have had with a guidance counselor, who has too many students to serve and is under-experienced in serving those who are not planning to follow the same stable professional route he himself followed.

Preparation for Work or Welfare

Our nation has accepted a challenge which has not been accepted by any nation or civilization since the dawning of time. We have set as a goal the job of eradicating poverty, enabling all persons in our nation to participate in the

American Dream. This goal comes headlong into conflict with the problem of welfare. The people on relief are not sharing in the American Dream; they are not participating in the productive capacity of our nation. Both the ethical and political motivations in our affluent society encourage this effort to eradicate poverty. To simplify the issue, there seem to be two approaches: 1) give the people on welfare a greater share of the available goods and servics, thus reducing the amount of goods and services available to the producers; 2) assist all of the able-bodied persons on welfare to become a part of the productive society, thus enabling them to have a greater share of the goods and services through their own abilities and their own production. The first approach would result in more and more people sharing less and less goods and services. Why should they work when they could enjoy the good life without the personal investment? The second factor is the only real answer if we wish to remain an independent, developing nation, rather than become a welfare state.

Welfare is the most pitiful experience in the history of this century. It is proven that it is not a solution, but part of the problem. In the State of Ohio, the legislature found it necessary in the 1969 session to appropriate more money to maintain the present inadequate welfare program at its present level for FY 1970 and FY 1971 than for the improvements in the system of public education. This massive welfare increase was necessary, even in the face of the lowest unemployment rate in the history of our state. The problems of welfare do not exist with the aged, the blind, and the infirm. These can be taken care of by an affluent society through changes in our social security system. The real problem comes with the A.D.C. families and the able-bodied persons on welfare. The answers to the welfare system do not start with attempts to train adults who have learned to live on welfare through several generations, but in the first grade with a system of vocational guidance based on the concept that work—all work —is honorable. The question of work being a vocation or just employment is a matter of attitude toward and commitment to work, not a function of the level of that employment.

Solutions Needed

The educational problem in the development of an adequate program of vocational guidance is closely tied to the problem discussed earlier in relationship to an antiquated curriculum. As the high school developed, the discipline-centered curriculum of the college was established in the high school as the educational curriculum, usurping the majority of the students' time in grades 9 through 12. The subject-centered curriculum of the high school was in turn imposed upon the junior high school as that segment of the educational program was developed. Efforts to integrate a broadened vocational guidance program, or a vocational education program into the educational system, immediately meet the problem of "We don't have time in the curriculum. If we change the curriculum we will interfere with the college preparatory offerings." As we watch developments at the national level I am convinced that the public schools will either accept the challenge for major changes in the educational system, or face a development of a competing parallel system for job training under the Department of Labor. The major guidance counselor system for adults now rests in the Department of Labor through the state employment services.

The crying need in our educational system is for massive changes in the curriculum and direction of our public education programs. Such changes are critical to the maintenance of our way of life. Such changes represent the only solutions to the social and economic problems that we face today. Yet what group has the understandings, the stature and the political expertise to bring about such changes in the educational system so badly needed at this point in the development of our nation? The needs of youth and adults cry out for relevance in our curriculum. Too often our answer has been to make the curriculum harder rather than more relevant.

There is no evidence that industry has the skills or knowledge or inclination to serve as an educational agency. Experiences with the Job Corps and with the National Alliance for Businessmen prove it would be an unusual case in which industry could divert sufficient time and energy from their primary and important function of production for profit to adequately serve the needs of an educational program. The federal government, through the Manpower programs, certainly has not shown that it has the ability to provide solutions to our social and economic problems even though massive amounts of dollars have been expended on those problems through the Office of Economic Opportunity and the Manpower Development and Training Acts. This is not to say that some continuing remedial functions of the Manpower programs are not necessary, but that none of these represent solutions. The only solutions rest in changed programs in our public schools; at the core of these changes must be an expanded system of vocational guidance and vocational education.

As we look to the immediate and long-range needs of our industries and businesses, we find that the over-emphasis upon the professional areas may soon leave us critically short of skilled personnel to keep our industries and businesses open. An economist from the Department of Labor, speaking at a Governor's Conference on Vocational and Technical Education in the spring of 1969, stated that if all economists were to drop dead tomorrow the economy would continue with hardly a ripple, but that if all tool-and-die makers were to drop dead tomorrow, the economy would come to a grinding halt within three weeks.[3] The increased salary level of the skilled employees in our businesses and industries has forced us to give some attention to their impact on the economy. We do not recognize, however, the amount of time and effort that must be expended to develop a skilled worker. It is impossible in six months to polish a person's manners, attitudes and work habits and hope to achieve a skilled worker. The jobs that are going to be available in our future will require people who know something and who can do something. There can be jobs for all. There must be jobs for all. But the people must be provided with the opportunity to prepare for such jobs.

---

[3] Robert M. Reese and Joseph K. Witteman, *A Governor's Symposium on Vocational Education* (Columbus: The Ohio State University, April, 1969), p. 128.

Current Limitations in Guidance
Programs in Our Public Schools

As the family no longer provides the op-
portunities to helping young people select their occupation through
experiences gained in the home or at the place of the father's
employment, a social vacuum is created. Schools began to experi-
ment with extending their curriculum beyond the normal college
preparatory curriculum as a significant number of students began
to finish high school who were not going on to college. In an
attempt to solve the problem forced upon them of assisting youth
in vocational choices, schools have too often assigned that responsibility to a guidance counselor. The program has become counselor-centered, rather than curriculum-centered. But there are too
few counselors to make an effective contribution and too many
of these counselors still offer only college-centered guidance.

The ratio of students to guidance counselor is several hundred to one in high school and even greater in junior high school.
Guidance counselors are rare in the elementary school. How can
guidance counselors function in their assigned role with so few to
serve so many?

The guidance and counseling program in too many of our
public schools has become a one-to-one relationship between
counselor and pupil, limited to those students with personal problems and those selecting colleges. Too many counselors subscribe
to the concise but comprehensive definition established by the
National Vocational Guidance Association in 1937, which states:
"Vocational guidance is the process of assisting the individual to
choose an occupation, prepare for it, enter upon it, and progress
in it."[4] They assume that the individual guidance counselor must
assume the major role, if not the total responsibility, and believe
that if they just get enough occupational information in written
handbooks or on computers they will be able to solve the problems
of all students. While this definition could be stretched to cover
almost any guidance program, it centers the guidance activities

---

[4] "Occupations," *The Vocational Guidance Magazine,* XV (May 1937), 772–
778.

around the counselor at a point in the high-school career of the student when he is ready to make a choice and limits the program to essentially occupational information.

A definition which encompasses a broader concept of a vocational guidance program was formulated by the U. S. Office of Education in 1939 as follows: "The process of acquainting the individual with various ways in which he may discover and use his natural endowment in addition to special training available from any source so that he may live and make a living to the best advantages to himself and society."[5] Dr. Donald Super, a contemporary leader in the field of guidance, suggests the following as a definition for a guidance program: "Vocational guidance is the process of helping a person to develop and accept an integrated and adequate picture of himself and of his role in the world of work, to test this concept against reality and to convert it into a reality with satisfaction to himself and benefit to society."[6]

Undoubtedly it would be possible to organize a total guidance program based upon any of these stated concepts of guidance. But all of these definitions seem to be based on the assumption of the "reason" approach in education, and ignore completely the place of emotion in occupational choice. Discussions with leaders in the field of guidance would indicate that much of the guidance research today is aimed at the development of better occupational information materials and improved delivery systems for impacting these materials upon people. The programs at workshops which I have addressed seem to be counselor-centered, rather than guidance-centered. People are not putty that can be molded; neither are they rugs that can be unfolded, so any program which is counselor-centered and limited to a year or two of the educational career of the person cannot be called a guidance program.

The term *vocational* in reference to guidance is looked upon as having reference to occupations which might be assumed to be a "calling". Some people prefer to use "career" guidance on the basis that careers hold more status and represent greater stability.

---

[5] Theodore Struck, *Vocational Education for a Changing World* (New York: John Wiley & Sons, Inc., 1945), p. 313.

[6] Robert Hoppock, *Occupational Information* (New York: McGraw-Hill Book Co., 1963), p. 96.

The term *occupational* is often used as an all-encompassing word to replace vocational. Occupational neither refers to a career of status and stability, nor a vocation which has the connotation of being a calling. The "occupation" concept of guidance suggests that a person may have a series of jobs requiring varying levels of skills. Still another group would suggest the use "employment" guidance in recognition that some of the jobs to which the youth would eventually aspire would really require no training and no skills. This attempt at identifying a hierarchy of jobs by the use of different types of terminology demeans all work. It has been my observation that a person in any level of work who respects himself and respects his services to mankind is entitled to have the pride of a calling. A person in a high profession may view his work as only a job; a person in a service occupation of low social status may view his work as a calling, as means of serving mankind. On the basis that any job can be a calling if a person invests himself in his work, I will continue to use the terms *vocational guidance* and *vocational education.*

Guidance counselors are essentially products of the last twenty years. The programs to prepare counselors at our universities and colleges are conceptually limited, stressing the areas of the guidance counseling function which would give the counselor greater status in the educational hierarchy. We find therefore that the terminology *vocational guidance* is often omitted from even the counselor education program at our universities. Emphasis is placed upon personal counseling, social counseling, educational counseling, with many counselors identifying themselves as quasi-psychologists or psychotherapists.

The problem was well illustrated when, at a national (AP-GA) meeting in Las Vegas, two meetings were scheduled simul-taneously. One meeting covered sensitivity training; the other, occupational information programming for major cities. The sensitivity training session had an overflow crowd, with people standing, while the session dealing with the occupational guidance information for major cities had five people on the program and drew an audience of three.

The training of guidance counselors does not include an understanding of a total system of vocational guidance, nor an understanding of the vocational education programming at the high school and post-high school levels which must serve as a tool for the vocational guidance program. The emphasis has been upon the training of guidance counselors, rather than upon the preparation of people to provide leadership to systems of vocational guidance. Even though guidance had its origin in the area of vocational guidance, the small number of guidance persons employed in the public schools have often been in the more affluent school districts. In these districts the influential mothers and fathers, representing the intellectually elite students, have encouraged the guidance counselors to spend a significant portion of their time assisting such students to select a college and preparing college transcripts. While this emphasis upon college guidance may have had self-satisfaction to counselors and may have made them feel secure in terms of assisting the students to follow along the same route that they have followed, I do not know of any guidance studies in which the guidance counselor was a significant factor in the selection of professional careers at colleges or universities.

Title V, the National Defense Education Act, provided for a broad expansion of the number of guidance counselors in the public schools of our nation. While there is ample evidence that the number of guidance counselors has been expanded, there is no evidence that there have been significant programs of vocational guidance established in any number of high schools served by those counselors. Our Division of Guidance and Testing reports that there are perhaps even fewer group guidance programs in the ninth-grade level than there were several years ago. Yet very few research studies show the guidance counselor as an important or effective functioning part of students' occupational choice or vocational programming. Likewise, I do not know of any research studies which have pointed up the guidance counselor as an effective psychologist, psychotherapist or of great importance in the maintenance of good pupil-school relationships.

Perhaps the limitations of the guidance program are centered in the very limited concepts of student services in which the guidance counselor himself, supplemented by paper and pencil, tests and written occupational information, constitutes the major resource of the guidance program. While written information about occupations may be important, I do not know of any studies which show that such material has ever helped youth to make decisions concerning themselves or occupations. It would seem feasible to suggest that studies be made of the effectiveness of such tools as occupational information pamphlets, computer centered occupational information, and other such informational tools before many millions of dollars are invested in them. Such techniques tend to ignore the social and economic backgrounds of the people, the emotions of the individual, the reading capabilities of the person involved, and the lack of personal relationship between the materials and the individual.

It would seem also that guidance personnel have been so concerned with the process of guidance that they have failed to take any responsibility or interest in the product. A superintendent in one medium-sized city asked his guidance counselors what percentage of students were going to college from the high schools. The guidance counselors proudly indicated that 60 percent of the students were attending college upon graduation. The superintendent then asked the guidance counselors what percentage of the students finished college. The counselors had no answer to this question. The superintendent's next comment was, "Are we giving . . . points to the counselors for the number of students that they send to college?"

An extensive research study conducted by the Center for Vocational and Technical Education of The Ohio State University and reported in December 1968 concerned vocational guidance in secondary education.

The need for a systematic approach to the redirection of the guidance program was stated in conclusions and recommendation as follows:

> The conclusion seems inescapable: if guidance programs are to be effective in meeting service needs with limited resources, they must be designed systematically and realistically to achieve a set of clearly stated objectives selected from a much larger set of possible objectives. As resources are increased, the set of stated objectives can be expanded as warranted by the resources. Further, methods for achieving the objectives must be designed or selected to accomplish their purpose efficiently; the choice cannot be restricted to meth-

ods previously used. This study did not provide an adequate basis for the selection of a set of universally appropriate objectives with a companion set of means for their accomplishment. But the task is feasible for any school, or other operating unit, through the general methods developed for designing and analyzing systems of many kinds.*

As indicated in the above extract, the study did not establish appropriate objectives or a system for achieving the objectives. The study did, however, identify some methods for consideration in the development of a guidance program. A summarization of these methods is as follows:

1. Team approach, using specialists, such as psychologists, nurses, teachers, etc.
2. A guidance role for teachers
3. A role for the para-professionals
4. Interagency cooperation
5. Use of data processing and computer technology
6. Student involvement in accepting responsibility for their plans and decisions
7. Involvement of the counselor in developing the school's curriculum
8. The development of exploratory programs
9. The use of advisory committees
10. Counselor education consistent with the planned program*

The methods suggested by the study focus almost entirely upon factors now outside the existing role of the guidance counselors. The focus upon teachers, curriculum, exploration programs and community involvement reflect some of the basic factors suggested in the system of vocational education and guidance proposed in this book.

Fully certificated guidance counselors have not typically been given training or experiences in community activities to become involved with the industries within their communities. Our modern

---

* Robert E. Campbell *et al., Vocational Guidance in Secondary Education* (Columbus: The Ohio State University, Center for Vocational and Technical Education, 1968), p. 175.
   * *Ibid.*

technology would suggest that students must not only have the benefit of a guidance system to help them in making occupational choices and the vocational, technical or professional education to help them become prepared for employment, but also a placement and follow-up program which would assure all youth of an opportunity for effective entrance into the labor force. It is satisfying to become the counselor involved in a guidance process, but the involvement in that process should also carry the responsibility for involvement with satisfactory adjustment of the product into society.

Guidance programs have almost universally ignored the area of post-secondary education, except as they have found it necessary to "recruit" students to initiate or maintain two-year post-high school technical education programs. The state employment services from the Department of Labor have almost universally become the centers for guidance and counseling for the dropouts, the unemployed and the under-employed. The state employment services, while supposedly less professionally trained than the guidance counselors in the public schools, have been engaged in assisting guidance counselors to obtain broader experiences in industry and business and with special groups such as disadvantaged youth. What is the future of the guidance programs in our public schools if they remain counselor-centered, paper-and-pencil centered, college-guidance centered and process-centered, and ignore the needs of most youth and adults for preparation for work through vocational and technical training?

SUMMARY

There are many forces pointing toward new concepts of guidance, including concepts of vocational guidance. The laws of our nation have tended to force youth to remain in school on the basis of denying them the opportunity to enter any significant employment in our economy. The laws of most states regulate against youth dropping out from school before the age of 16 and many states have regulations which prevent students from dropping out of school before the age of 18 or completion of the high school curriculum. In many cases if schools would only meet their responsibilities in law, there would be few students under the age of 18 out of school and out of work. I see no basis for a school to drop a student who has not achieved a diploma or completed a vocational education program which prepares him for economic self-sufficiency. Public schools can no longer unload their problems and failures onto the public.

The cry for relevancy in our curriculum brings to light the inadequacies of our present curriculum and encourages experimentation and change in the total educational program. The social dynamite identified by Dr. James Conant in a study made in 1961 has exploded in the sections of our major cities in which the social and economic problems prevented them from participating in a way of life which they see daily on television. Our public schools must radically change or be by-passed as a significant factor in the development of our nation.

As we face the re-orientation of our educational system, it is very possible that the development of a system of vocational guidance and vocational education can bring about the development of a sub-system in the educational program, reaching from kindergarten throughout the work life of the individual. Throughout the nation we are experiencing a rapid growth of vocational and technical education programs at the high school and post-high school levels as alternatives to the college-preparatory and baccalaureate collegiate programs. The support for the development of these programs by business, industry, the public, and educational leadership would indicate that the programs may be made available more rapidly than the parents and students are prepared to take advantage of them.

Jobs, not welfare, are the answer to our social and economic problems. The welfare system is bankrupt. It demeans the persons receiving it, condemns them to a life as secondary citizens, and imposes an increasing burden upon the person working for a living. The solution to our problem rests in preparing people for jobs before they leave a full-time educational program at the high school, post-high school or collegiate level. For most young people, however, the high school is their last opportunity for a full-time educational program. Youth at the age of 16 become goal-oriented and recognize the fact that their future is closely tied with their ability to do well some phase of work of the world. The present and projected growth of vocational education programming as a solution to social and economic problems provides vocational guidance with a massive opportunity to participate in the total program.

Mature leadership has been evolving in the area of guidance as this new area in the field of education comes of age. Additional research in the field of guidance can provide information and encouragement to move from the counselor-centered activities to the system-centered activities. To find itself, guidance must lose itself within the educational program. The guidance counselor must see himself, not as *the* guidance program, but as a specialist who helps with the development of the program.

Chapter 2   FORCES SHAPING VOCATIONAL GUIDANCE

Social Forces

In the face of competition for the tax dollar, money is going to flow to the segment of the educational community which produces results—results in terms of the social and economic problems that we face and not results in terms of how many took Latin. A governor of a neighboring state, at a Conference of Mid-western Governors, told the conference that he was tired of pouring money down a rathole of increasing educational costs without seeing any change in the educational process or product.

It is possible that the educational program today has been allowed to stay one hundred years out of date because of the nostalgic relationship of the program to the adults who look back to their "good old school days." Youth presently enrolled in our schools are more mature and more discriminating concerning their educational services than we were some years ago. The scope of the educational services being demanded of public education can

be determined somewhat from the statement of the purpose of the
Vocational Education Act of 1963, Public Law 88-210, passed by
the U.S. Congress.

> authorized federal grants to states to assist them to main-
> tain, extend and approve existing programs of vocational
> education, to develop new programs of vocational educa-
> tion, and to provide part-time employment for youths who
> need the earnings from such employment to continue their
> vocational training on a full-time basis, so that persons of
> all ages in all communities of the State—those in high
> school, those who have completed or discontinued their
> formal education and are preparing to enter the labor mar-
> ket, those who have already entered the labor market but
> need to upgrade their skills or learn new ones, and those
> with special educational handicaps—will have ready access
> to vocational training or retraining which is of high qual-
> ity, which is realistic in the light of actual or anticipated op-
> portunities for gainful employment, and which is suited to
> their needs, interests, and ability to benefit from such train-
> ing.

This act encouraged significant expansion of vocational guidance programs and was updated in the Vocational Education
Amendments of 1968 (PL 90-576) to encourage the use of vocational education funding for *vocational* guidance and a cooperative working relationship between vocational education and
vocational guidance.

It seems to me that it is also significant that at the national
level, funding under Title V of the National Defense Education
Act for guidance is in trouble. Even the limited amount of funds
provided under Title V of the National Defense Education Act
were not recommended in the President's budget for inclusion in
the appropriation of Congress, even though Congress subsequently
inserted funding at the same level as available in a preceding year.
At the state level, our legislature has not seen fit to fund guidance
counselors as a significant part of the school foundation program,
except that the 1969 session of the legislature did provide $400,-
000 to the Division of Vocational Education for the expansion
of *vocational* guidance. I believe it is very possible that the guidance movement has become a captive of the theoreticians at the

university level who gain their recognition in the academic community by the involvement of new theories and concepts, rather than by the development of practical, meaningful programs in the public schools. Leadership must rest with practical people in positions of responsibility in our state departments of education. The professional personnel in guidance in our universities and colleges have a very important function to serve. I question, however, whether they are motivated or qualified to give the kind of leadership suggested in an integrated program of vocational guidance and vocational education.

Mounting Public Pressure for Change

In my report to the State legislature on February 5, 1969, I referred to *A Report by the Governor's Task Force on Vocational and Technical Education;* this task force had been appointed prior to the opening of the legislature to make recommendations which could be translated into legislation. The report, I believe, is a forward-looking and historical document which recommended educational changes which would make a significant improvement in services to youth and adults. The Task Force, in considering the concerns of one state, noted these items:

1. There are 30,000 dropouts and forceouts a year. Every five years this adds at least 150,000 untrained, unskilled and largely unemployable persons to the labor market.
2. Of the unemployed in Ohio, 83 percent are under 35 years of age.
3. Of these unemployed, 50 percent did not finish high school.
4. Nearly 50 percent completed high school, but still cannot find work.
5. Of Ohio's unemployed young people, 28 percent never held a job.[1]

---

[1] *A Report by the Governor's Task Force on Vocational and Technical Education* (State of Ohio, January, 1969).

The Task Force in its report suggested the following guidelines for an employment-oriented program, which I am designating in this book as a system of vocational guidance and vocational education:

A. The needs of the individual student.
B. The needs of the local community.
C. Adequate student testing, evaluation and counseling.
D. Placement services for students and graduates.
E. Provisions for special programs for special cases.
F. Instructors must have had recent employment in the fields in which they are teaching.
G. Before graduation the student should do actual work in the field he is studying through a local employer.
H. Industry and employers must cooperate closely with the schools, both in forming the necessary programs and in implementing them.
I. A realistic minimum class size and number of units offered must be set.
J. Educational television and computerized teaching can be invaluable tools in this type of teaching. They would be utilized to the fullest extent possible.[2]

The Task Force recommended an employment-oriented education or system of vocational guidance and vocational education from the first grade through high school as follows:

First Six Grades
    1. Respect for the world of work
    2. Motivation to want to do some part of the world of work
Grades Seven and Eight
    Career orientation of all students to our technological society
Grades Nine and Ten
    1. Exploration for occupational choice
    2. Work adjustment program for school-disoriented youth

[2] *Ibid.*

Grades Eleven and Twelve (sixteen years of age and up)
Broad, goal-centered educational programs
Post-High School
1. Technical Education
2. Professional Education
3. Retraining of unemployed and upgrading of employed adults[3]

The implementation of such suggestions would amount to a revolution in the field of education, since such changes could not take place and maintain the existing, narrowly-conceived, subject-centered, discipline-oriented curriculum. The Task Force indicated that if any progress was to be made towards the recommendations of their report that all leaders must accept and disseminate these truths:

Learning to work and working to earn are basic human rights.

Learning a trade, skill, occupation or craft is just as worthy as learning a profession.

Most jobs today and almost all new jobs in the future will require some skill acquired through formal training.

Industrial growth will grind to a stop if skilled workers are not at hand to perform the necessary jobs.[4]

The members of this Task Force were from business, industry, education, and government and were experiencing the technological forces that must be recognized in shaping the system of vocational guidance and vocational education for the future. They knew that most jobs in the future would require training prior to entry. They knew about the shortage of skilled workers. They knew about skilled workers as a creative force in our technological society, and they knew that business and industry would have

---

[3] *Ibid.*
[4] *Ibid.*

increasing dependence upon the public educational services. The people represented on this Task Force were fully aware of the sociological forces impacting upon our educational system. They recognized that welfare rolls were increasing in a period of time in which we had the lowest unemployment rate of any period in the history of our state. They joined with me in the concept that welfare has no answers; that it is part of the problem, not part of the solution. The Task Force recognized that because of our low rates of unemployment for the total population, personnel for the growth of their industries and businesses, for the growth of our social organizations and institutions, must come from the youth graduating from our high schools, technical institutes and colleges.

There is high unemployment for youth in the face of many excellent job openings. In any major city newspaper there are pages of want ads for people, but they want people with skills and technical knowledge, not just a strong back. Youth out of school and out of work represent a dangerous force, particularly in our major cities. I believe sincerely that we will either prepare these youth for work and provide them with jobs, or we will continue to fight them in the streets. The Task Force realized that economic forces that impinge upon our nation must also be recognized and have an impact upon our educational system.

The elimination of low-paying jobs is necessary because such jobs do not pay a living wage and welfare payments are often above that wage level. Many jobs which are low-paying now must be upgraded by improving the productivity of workers through training to the point where such jobs can be paid a living wage. Increased productivity is the only basis for increased earnings. Earnings tied to any other base only cheapen our money and increase inflation. The causes of poverty are basically lack of jobs and job training and a lack of motivation to reach out for the jobs and job training that are available. People on our poverty rolls could be changed within ten years from an economic liability to an economic asset if they became a part of the producers of goods and services, rather than consumers of tax dollars.

The Blunt Facts

A study completed by the Employment Service in Ohio proved that 89.4 percent of the youth searching for employment had absolutely no skills to offer an employer. Jobs need people, and people need jobs. Projected from our experience in Ohio, the nation annually dumps into the labor market two million young people whose only qualifications are willingness to work. This group includes dropouts from high school, dropouts from college, and graduates from high school who do not have vocational training and do not continue their education.[5] Our state employment service indicates that two-thirds of our unemployment in the nation represents youth between the ages of 16 and 21. For negro youth, the unemployment rate is more than twice the rate for white workers. The unemployment rate for Negro teenagers, identified at 26.5 percent, was not appreciably lower in 1967 than during the recession-affected year of 1961. In fact, the differences between unemployment rates of non-white teenagers and those of white teenagers has increased. The unemployment rate for white teenagers dropped as the economic climate improved, but the rate among non-white teenagers in 1967 was higher than in previous years. The unemployment rate for the non-white teenagers was almost two and a half times the proportion for white teenagers, whereas in 1960 the ratio was less than two to one. In 1966 the non-white unemployment rate in some areas of large cities among 14 to 19 year olds ranged from 18.4 percent in Washington, D.C. to 36 percent in Philadelphia.[6]

Non-whites need to gain access to white collar and skilled jobs at a faster rate than they have in recent years. The door to gain access to the white collar and skilled jobs is the door of vocational and technical education, not power politics or violence.

---

[5] Figures based on the survival rate of the 1968 graduating class, and 1966 projections of rates of collegiate enrollments and survivals to graduation, Ohio State Department of Education and the Board of Regents.

[6] *Vocational Training, Employment and Unemployment, Part I, National Trends,* U.S. Department of Health, Education, and Welfare (Washington, D.C.: U.S. Office of Education, January, 1969).

A review of national trends indicates that despite the greater openings in jobs in some occupations, employment opportunities for non-whites are predominantly in the low-income and low-skilled occupations. Industries with a declining employment rate normally include the industries which have traditionally employed the Negro. Attention must be given to the needs of all youth, and particular attention must be given to the training needs of the non-white population.

Parents and Public

Efforts to make educational changes in the curriculum face a difficult time in breaking down the resistance of the parents to any program that does not have the status of university preparation. It is obvious that the guidance counselor is not the cause of the preoccupation of youth with the college preparatory curriculum, but it might be fair to ask, "What has the guidance profession done to overcome the attitudes of youth and parents regarding the 'acceptable' occupations?" The real hope for change in parents, the public, and youth rests with the news media. Radio, television, and newspapers must make massive efforts to reflect the growing concerns on the part of the industry and government for a massive revision of our educational system to provide for a meaningful system of vocational guidance and vocational education. Vocational education must develop the necessary materials for public-service time on radio and television. In most cases professionals are needed to develop the type of material that has an impact on the public. Amateur productions will receive little attention on the part of radio and television producers.

The newspapers, however, represent the most important method of reaching the public. They will publish news, but will not give time and attention to informative items of limited interest. It is important to remember that a public-information program is much broader than a publicity program. Publicity is important, but it cannot be a substitute for sound programs and personal efforts of all of the people working in the program.

An editorial in the January 9, 1970 issue of *The Columbus*

Dispatch is an example of the type of journalism that is needed to effect changes in our system:

> Ohio's rate of unemployment, running about a full percentage point below the national average, should not be viewed with complacency. Rather it is an insured challenge to convert our idle, virtually all unskilled, into potential employables.
>
> A recent yearend report by William Papier, research director for the Ohio Bureau of Employment Services, put the state's unemployment rate at 2.7 percent of the state's labor force, compared to a national average of 3.5 percent.
>
> At the same time, Mr. Papier declared that "literally thousands of jobs have gone begging for lack of qualified candidates." He listed myriad job openings in both blue collar and white collar classifications.
>
> Paul W. McCracken, chairman of President Nixon's Council of Economic Advisers, has predicted there may be "fairly sluggish business activity" during the first half of this new year and a pickup in the latter half.
>
> And what will spark the upturn? Mr. McCracken expects the pickup to be reflected mainly in housing and in state and local projects.
>
> In other words, there will be an increasing need for workers right here at home, for Ohio ranks near the top among states which enjoy a steadily expanding economy in both the public and private sectors.
>
> But we are now in the doldrums of the off-season when parts of our economy, such as building, are at low ebb. A little farther up the road is the end of the school year when a fresh batch of our youth will be available on the labor market.
>
> Now is the time to take inventory of our idle labor supply and make sure they do not become permanently idled because of lack of job know-how.
>
> Government, education and business leaders and parents must redouble their preachings against school dropouts, lest they, too, swell the ranks of our unskilled idle.
>
> Because Ohio's leaders have been progressive and alert to the state's vast and diversified potential, we have kept our idle rate low. The difference between the Ohio and national idle rates is a commendable buffer and should be used to assure continuance of this state's steady growth over the last several years.

Students

Students are maturing earlier. The 18-year old of yesterday is a 16-year old today. The news media, the world of technology, the changes in social mores, all combine to let youth mature earlier in terms of knowledge and understanding of the world in which they live. As young people in an affluent nation, they are involved, disturbed, guilty, scared; they feel unneeded and look perhaps with awe and with some fear upon a society which demands so much of those wanting to enter the world of work and offers so little to them as a means of preparing for that world of work. One-fourth of all the youth in Ohio drop out before graduating from high school. One publication identified the educational experiences of these youth as follows:

> The school day is long and tedious. The education they are receiving seems to lack relevance to their future life and needs. The school sytsem often fails to recognize and respect their culturally different backgrounds. Some teachers lack an understanding of their special needs and problems, or ignore them. Little or no special instruction and attention are provided which might help them fit into the regular school programs. Too much school time, in their view, is spent on discipline; staff members are occasionally involved in physical conflict with the students. Such behavior on the part of adults is already too frequent a part of these youngsters' lives. They think they are not given the type of counseling, encouragement, or other support they need to enter the world of work, and so they leave school unprepared for a job. When they encounter discrimination or failure in job seeking because of their age, race, or poor educational background, they do not believe that a return to school will improve their situation.[7]

The pressures for high achievement are enormous. The penalties for under-achievement are terrible. The opportunities in vocational guidance and vocational education, particularly for

---

[7] Barbara H. Kemp, *The Youth We Haven't Served*, U.S. Dept. of Health, Education, and Welfare (Washington, D.C.: 1966).

those on the low end of the social and economic scale, are almost non-existent. I truly wonder if the disruptive youth who violently protest against the Establishment and who can clearly point up many of the problems existing in our civilization are idealistic or just scared. We live in an age of the non-hero hero for the minority of youth who fear the competition of a technological world. Charlie Brown is the hero of the "cop out," the "hippie," that minority of the youth of our nation, who are busy pointing out the faults of that nation, but who do not have any time to lend their efforts, through continuing work, to build it to greater services to mankind.

One out of every four persons is in a public school, private or parochial school, technical institute, college or university, or some phase of an educational program. Education is big business —perhaps the biggest business in the nation. What right does this system have to maintain a curriculum irrelevant to the needs of most of the youth and to have this curriculum contribute to student unrest? The lack of relevancy in the curriculum is not restricted to the high-school program. It is just as important a force in the youth disturbances on the collegiate level.

Youth, when given an opportunity free from external pressure to express their interests are interested in training for a job. They are much more realistic regarding their futures than is the educational curriculum in which they are enrolled, or the projections made regarding college enrollments. Evidence to support this concept was obtained during February of 1969, when approximately 40,000 students in grades 8 through 12 took part in the national standardization of the Ohio Vocational Interest Survey (OVIS). OVIS is a new interest inventory designed to assist students in Grades 8 through 12 with their educational and vocational planning. The standardization sample was selected from ten regions of the United States and included forty-three school systems from the following states: Alabama, California, Colorado, Iowa, Massachusetts, North Carolina, Ohio, Oregon, Pennsylvania and Texas. The summary of one part of that study, listed below, shows that 74 to 76 percent of the students in Grades 8 through 12 consistently indicated they were interested in or were already enrolled in vocational education.

INTEREST IN VOCATIONAL PROGRAM

Grade	8		9		10	
	Number	%	Number	%	Number	%
TOTALS	5087		5144		4696	
1. Already Enrolled	45	1	599	12	879	19
2. Interested	3867	76	3387	57	2686	57
3. Not Interested	1148	23	1146	22	1122	24
OMITS	27	1	12	0	9	0

Grade	11		12		Total	
	Number	%	Number	%	Number	%
TOTALS	4317		3953		23197	
1. Already Enrolled	1361	32	1417	36	4301	19
2. Interested	1911	44	1487	38	13338	57
3. Not Interested	1032	24	1040	26	5488	24
OMITS	13	0	9	0	70	0

Growth of Guidance Programs

The National Vocational Guidance Association was first organized in Grand Rapids, Michigan on October 24, 1913. By 1945 the membership of the organization had increased to 3000, and at the time the National Defense Education Act was passed in 1958, the organization had a membership of 6811. The effect of the Title V of the National Defense Education Act upon the guidance programs in this nation can be evaluated when we find that the NVGA now has a membership of 9774 members. The growth of guidance counselors as members of the educational team is a positive indication that our educational system recognizes the need to accept a responsibility for vocational guidance. Too often, however, counselors are hired to develop a guidance program but are not given the administrative assistance or direction they need. Instead they are fettered with numerous menial duties in the pupil personnel area, such as attendance work. Few are employed specifically as vocational guidance counselors. Even fewer make any strong effort to develop a vocational guidance program.

Before the passage of the National Defense Education Act, state leadership in guidance was kept alive by vocational education funds. Persons responsible for programming in vocational education have long recognized the importance of a combined system of vocational guidance and vocational education and have been willing to invest the limited funds made available to them. The Vocational Education Act of 1963, P.L. 88-210, encouraged the use of vocational education funds to expand a vocational guidance program in the various states. The encouragement of vocational funding for guidance programs was continued as a part of the Vocational Education Act of 1968, P.L. 90-576, growing out of the report of the National Committee on Vocational Education.

School superintendents and others report that where personnel are employed specifically in vocational guidance they have made a positive and significant contribution to the development of vocational guidance programs at the high-school level, complementing and making effective use of the vocational education programs in those schools. In our state, the Division of Vocational Education is paying a part of the salaries for 152 vocational guidance counselors. This number of counselors was *added* to the counseling staffs for the specific purpose of vocational guidance. On the basis of the success of the vocational guidance counselors, our state legislature has provided an additional $400,-000 for the employment of vocational counselors during the 1970–71 school year.

SUMMARY

Technological forces, social forces and economic forces all point towards increased emphasis upon the preparation of youth for entrance into employment. These factors point up that effective participation in a technological society demands a price; that price is preparation for work at either the high school, the post-high school or the collegiate level. The facts indicate that most of the people in our state and in the nation will earn their living in occupations other than those requiring a college degree. In 1960, 92 out of every 100 people above the age of 21 in Ohio earned their living without a college degree. It is projected that 88 out of every 100 in 1970 will be earning their living without such a degree.

The attitudes of the parents, educators and general public, encourage the maintenance of an educational program that is currently out of date and forces young people into educational programs and educational choices wrong for them and wrong for our nation. Too many parents tell their young people, "Don't worry about what you want to do until you get out of high school, then make up your mind." For most young people, high school is their last chance for a full-time education. Even in a major western state, where post-high school education is free, less than 50 percent of the high school youth go on to full-time post-high school education. It is time to encourage choice and a commitment on the part of youth to make wise occupational choices and to participate in a relevant job-training program at the high school, post-high school or collegiate level.

Guidance services are relatively new in the public schools. Federal funding under the National Defense Education Act provided a stimulus for the growth of such services. The future of the guidance program, however, may rest more with the ability of the guidance profession to see that all youth are provided with guidance services than the provision of such services by the profession.

The future of a nation rests in the character of its youth. I am forever thankful that the large majority of the youth in our state and nation are decent, law-abiding people, and yet have a commitment to change and improvement through work. I am thankful that most young people are willing to commit their talents to this task, rather than demanding instant perfection in a very imperfect world. The world needs their heads and their hands to support the ideals they profess.

Chapter 3

CURRICULUM: BASIS FOR A VOCATIONAL GUIDANCE PROGRAM

Experience-Centered Guidance

Reading about occupations is of no more help to a boy or girl in choosing an occupation than reading about swimming is to a person who is in danger of drowning.

We don't expect people to choose marriage partners by reading lists of the traits of those available. How then can we expect that all a youngster needs to choose his life's occupation is a well-developed set of occupational information materials? Only a few exceptional people are able to make an effective transfer of learning from the abstract to the concrete without accompanying experiences. Reading about occupations is only one of many experiences needed for vocational choice, and not even the essential one.

Early philosophers in the field of education, such as Pestelozzi, Rousseau, and Froebel all came to the conclusion that to be effective, education, even at the elementary level, had to be centered in the *experience* of the person. It was for the reason of making education experience-centered that some of the early philosophers provided that the young person would be in school one-half day and at home working for one-half day. There was no intent to provide work experience as a basis for vocational training but as a basis for the learning of reading, writing and arithmetic in the school.

Psychological studies establishing principles of learning likewise have indicated the importance of "doing" as a basis for learning. Consider some of the psychological principles of learning:

1. We learn best when we are ready to learn. When we have a strong purpose, a well-fixed reason for learning something, it is easier to receive the instruction and to make progress in learning.
2. The more often we use what we have learned the better we can perform or understand it.
3. If the things we have learned are useful and beneficial to us, so that we are satisfied with what we have accomplished, the better we retain what we have learned.
4. Learning something new is made easier if the learning can be built upon something we already know. It is best to start with simple steps which are related to things we can now do or which we already understand, and proceed to new and more difficult tasks or ideas.
5. Learning takes place by doing. Before the learning can become complete, we must put into practice what we are attempting to learn.[1]

John Dewey made popular the phrase, "Learn by doing!" The studies of the early philosophers in education and the psychological experimentation in learning tend to suggest that experience is not only the best teacher, experience may be the *only* teacher. Since the reason for including vocational guidance in the public school is that experiences can no longer be obtained in the home setting, it would follow that for any vocational guidance system to be effective in the public school, it must also be experience-centered. Any curriculum which is not based upon experience will fail to serve the students and will fail in proportion to the lack of those experiences supplementing the classroom instruction. A student who comes from a home which provides a broad base of

---

[1] Gerald Leighbody, *Methods of Teaching Shop and Related Subjects* (Albany, N.Y.: Delmar Publishers, Inc., 1955), pp. 2–3.

experience essential to the learning process is not as handicapped as a student who comes from a home with very limited experience. A student who comes from a home with a low socio-economic base often has a greater handicap in the learning process than a student from a more affluent home. Therefore, the responsibility for filling the void caused by handicaps must be built into the curriculum.

I am proposing that the vocational guidance and vocational education system be an integral part of the total educational system and thus an integral part of the curriculum at all stages and educational levels of the program. Under this plan, the curriculum must provide the basis for the experiences necessary to provide an effective vocational guidance program. Work itself is a great teacher; it teaches responsibility, respect for the rights and privileges of others, the importance of economical use of time and the consequences of poor work or no work. Work-centered curricula should therefore be considered as a part of a system of vocational guidance and vocational education at differing levels in the public education system from kindergarten throughout the twelve grades of school.

Experience-Centered Core Curriculum

Youth rebellion begins for some youth the first day they attend the public school. Often this rebellion is indicated only in withdrawal from the group and failure to participate in the educational program. How relevant is our elementary education program to many of the youth coming from poverty-stricken homes? How relevant are Dick, Jane, and Spot to millions of youth who start to school in this nation? Vocational guidance and vocational education as a sub-system of the total education program can be made relevant at all age and grade levels. Or it can be made meaningless.

Research in the field of guidance shows that youth at an early age have an interest in occupations. Research by Gunn[2] has indicated that up to about 10 years of age students do not rank

---

[2] Barbara Gunn, "Children's Conceptions of Occupational Prestige," *Personnel and Guidance Journal,* XLII (February, 1964), 558–63.

occupation in any stable or meaningful way. At ages 11 or 12, or fourth and fifth grade, they show an ability to rank occupations, but use a service or social usefulness value base in doing so and still tend to see all jobs in a favorable light. Gunn's research indicates that youth begin to rank jobs by their status-conferring base by the time they are seventh graders. By the time they reach the tenth grade they view occupations in much the same way as do adults. Gunn has found that occupational aspirations can be one of the major components in stimulating activities of youth at all age levels, yet guidance has tended to relate the functions of the guidance counselor and whatever guidance program might be available to the high school years.

An analysis of achievement motivation by Rosen[3] indicated that educational occupational aspiration was one of the three major proponents of achievement-oriented behavior. Children learn about prestige stereotypes of occupations from the general culture even if the public education system does little formally or deliberately to assist youth with such understanding. Youth are learning by accident or by the prejudicial attitudes of their parents or their peers. Most of their attitudes on work are solidly formed long before the guidance program has any impact.

Reorganization of the curriculum to bring about relevance in education will require change not only at the high school level, but a change from the kindergarten on through the educational life of the student. If the research is accurate, and youth are interested and impressionable in terms of occupations in the early elementary years, why shouldn't the system of vocational guidance and vocational education begin at the earliest time that youth is exposed to the organized educational process?

To be more meaningful, curriculum organization should take the form of "core" curriculum. Dr. Harold B. Alberty developed the core curriculum in answer to an eight-year study in which he and Dr. Boyd H. Bode, then professors at The Ohio State University, participated between 1932 and 1941. The results of the study pointed up the fallacy of an established set of subjects as college

---

[3] Julius Rosen, *Job Values of Educationally Disadvantaged Students* (Associated Educational Services Corp., Simon & Schuster, Inc., 1968), p. 68.

entrance requirements.[4] The core curriculum is one in which the sharp lines between the subject fields disappear entirely or become blurred to the point of extinction. The curriculum is based on the life experiences of the students. Many areas of social, civic or educational concern can serve as a basis for the reading, writing and arithmetic to be taught in the elementary school. In the social demands approach to the core curriculum as described in the second volume of the report on eight years' study, one of the identified areas of human activities and problems of life is that of "getting a living"—vocations, maintenance, production, distribution, consumption, economy, labor, occupation, industry, unemployment, work capital, wealth, income.[5]

Recognizing the interest of youth in occupations and the motivations that the world of work can have for young people, work can be used as a central theme for a core of instruction adjusted to the age and grade level of the youth involved, moving from motivation to work, to learning about work and to preparing for work. Such a core program approach provides an educational base to insert a system of vocational guidance and vocational education into the main stream of the educational program.

I am not an educator. It does make sense to me, however, that *experience* must be at the heart of the educational process and that a system of vocational guidance and vocational education can become an integral part of such an experience-centered curriculum effort. Only the intellectually gifted can gain any significant understandings from reading about or hearing about the very fundamental thing that is going to occupy the majority of their life. Most of us, as John Dewey admonishes, "learn by doing."

The Teacher in Guidance

Little is said in guidance literature about the teacher and the curriculum in the guidance program. The emphasis is on the guidance counselor and stacks of written occupational information in pamphlets, on tapes, on computer-assisted

---

[4] Giles, McCutchen, Zechiel, *Exploring the Curriculum* (New York: Harper & Bros., 1942).

[5] *Ibid.*

programming and on films. I would suggest that the teachers, who are in daily contact with the students, do more positive or negative vocational guidance by accident than the vocational guidance counselors do by intent.

Almost unconsciously the teachers tend to direct the attention of students to the area of the professions since they, after all, are professionals. Just how effective is the school teacher as part of a guidance program when he tells a young person, "If you don't study hard you won't get into a good college and you will have to work for a living"? This type of guidance is an unconscious approach; most youth will not even realize that they have been affected by the teacher or the teacher's attitude, since at no time do the teachers say, "Now we are going to become part of the vocational guidance program and study occupations."

On the other hand, many persons have found a vocational interest because of the influence of one teacher; a teacher who cared, a teacher who motivated, a teacher who led them to invest themselves in a field of work. I doubt that many guidance studies related to occupational choice could identify the teacher as a significant single factor in occupational choice. It is very probable, however, that the total impact of teacher attitude from kindergarten on plays a significant part in the attitude of students toward occupations and the unwise choice of many in selecting the professions as their goal.

The almost total lack of concern for the curriculum and for the teacher on the part of the guidance professional is pointed up by H. B. Gelatt in the *Review of Educational Research* when he lists the needs of guidance personnel:

1. Non-professional support personnel are necessary.
2. Guidance schools and research must be related to the total educational system.
3. Guidance information research can contribute to guidance content.
4. Guidance research must directly involve students and guidance workers.
5. Guidance services and research must be innovative.[6]

---

[6] H. B. Gelatt, "School Guidance Programs," *Review of Educational Research,* Vol. 39, No. 2 (April, 1969), 149–51.

Even if all of these needs were met, there still would not be a guidance program without involving the curriculum and the teachers. As quarterback of the team, the trained guidance counselor can't win the game without the cooperation and coordination of the teachers.

The Importance of Student Success

A person's self-concept is important not only to his achievements, but to his satisfaction as a voyager through life. The academic, college preparatory curriculum in our public schools contributes mainly to the self-concept of the intellectually gifted. To a certain extent it measures the intellectual capacity of those participating, but such intellectual capacity can be measured more cheaply and better through the various intelligence quotient tests which measure the same kind of intelligence. But neither the academic curriculum nor the academically oriented intelligence test has been able to measure the kind of intelligence exhibited by Edison, Firestone, Chrysler, Ford and others who have made massive contributions to our economy. We hold before our youth the sacred banner of academic excellence as the only path toward success, and we measure success in terms of academic degrees and status positions within our community.

Students and workers, given an opportunity to express their needs and interests, often state them in terms of what they believe to be the socially accepted mores of the society, having been conned into believing that academic achievement is the measure of success. All through their school life, they have seen the accolades and attention and approbation go to the "A" students, so they respond in terms of the affluent society to which they hope to aspire, rather than in relationship to their own realistic goals and needs. The overwhelming assumption in our educational system seems to be that intelligence and social contribution come only from the college graduate. The absurdity of this is well expressed in a recent article by the celebrated national columnist, Alice Widener, after Stanford Ovshinsky had made a significant scientific breakthrough in the area of transistors. The article read as follows:

Names make news, and this month the name Stanford
R. Ovshinsky is making worldwide headlines.

Mr. Ovshinsky is the 46-year-old American inventor
of the newly announced "Ovshinsky Effect" in energy conversion, a discovery opening a new field in basic physics
and comparable to discoveries that led to invention, 21 years
ago, of the transistor.

Perhaps, Mr. Ovshinsky's human achievement is even
more significant than his marvelous scientific one. He has
knocked into a cocked hat, once and for all, the notion that
every boy or girl should go to college and cannot otherwise
achieve social and intellectual status. Stanford Ovshinsky
never saw the inside of a college.

In Akron, Ohio, he attended John R. Buchtel High
School daytimes and went to Hower Vocational School at
night as a machinist. He had a "C" average in academic
studies. He paid $5 tuition for a 12-week trade school course
of 48 hours. Three such courses were offered by Hower
Vocational School per year, and young Ovshinsky took them
for three years. His total trade school tuition amounted to
about $45. After graduation from high school, he opened up
a little machine shop in what one of his Akron teachers
describes as "a sort of chicken coop."

In an exclusive telephone interview, I asked inventor
Ovshinsky what helped him most in trade school. Without a
moment's hesitation, he replied firmly: "I learned how to
discipline myself to do work."

In himself, Ovshinsky is living proof of the falsity of
most shibboleths preached by contemporary intellectuals pro-
moting the notion that today no boy or girl can "make it" or
achieve status without going to college.

In himself, Mr. Ovshinsky is living proof that it is possible in 1968, as it was in 1848, and as it will be in 2048,
let us pray, for an American to make a Horatio Alger-type
success. Perhaps the greatest lesson to be learned from the
Ovshinsky achievement is that it was done in the very field
where most contemporary academic educators say it posi-
tively could not be done—that is, the field of ultra-modern
science.

Now, perhaps, the intellectually snobbish academic op-
ponents of vocational-technical education will be less aggres-
sive.

Mr. Ovshinsky's invention probably has enabled every
Mom and Dad to have a flat, inexpensive television set, hung
like a picture on the living room wall. His human achieve-

ment ought to enable all, regardless of race, color or creed, to escape from the authoritarian tyranny of a purely academic-oriented school system.

The name of inventor Ovshinsky ought to become a nationwide symbol of hope and encouragement to parents and to young people. He has proved that today any boy or girl can go to trade or vocational school and achieve any degree of self-education desired. Stanford R. Ovshinsky also has proved that the best path to intellectual, material, and spiritual success for any young person is to learn how to acquire self-discipline "to do work."[7]

Our system tends to make most people feel inferior to a few. A study of the 1960 census data in Ohio indicated that only 7.6 percent of our people in the state were employed in the professions and that 4 percent of that 7.6 percent were in the area of education. If only this small percentage of the people end up in the professional area, does this mean that the rest of the people are failures? If so, then the future of our nation rests with the failures.

If a system of vocational guidance and vocational education is to succeed, all youth must have a favorable self-concept. Experience with disadvantaged youth indicates that those who have developed a favorable self-concept can go much farther in their work careers than was originally judged. Likewise, educationally mentally retarded students, when given a favorable self-concept and adequate learning time where they are not in competition with students of higher intelligence, can achieve into some semi-skilled and skilled occupations.

SUMMARY

Students should be able to meet with great success in a vocational guidance and vocational education system if their peers, teachers and parents judge their pursuits worthwhile and important

---

[7] *Columbus Dispatch,* November 19, 1968.

to society. I see no dichotomy in insisting that the system of vocational education and vocational guidance be an integral part of the total educational process, since skill in the basic tool subjects is essential to success in almost any field of work, not only in the professions. Actually, in some of the low-level jobs, the ability to read and write may be the only skills required of the person. Reversing this process, we find that for many young people, a relationship to occupational goals is essential if reading, writing and arithmetic are to have any meaning to them. In Ohio's Mahoning Valley Vocational Center, organized to provide skills and occupations for unemployed, out-of-school youth, students did not resist learning to read and write when the reading and writing instruction was related to their vocational training.

All youth can be successful at something. It is the job of the educational system to find this area of success and to develop abilities, not to point out shortcomings and failures. The total curriculum grades K-12 can serve as the basis for a system of vocational guidance and vocational education.

Chapter 4

RESOURCES FOR THE DEVELOPMENT OF A NEW SYSTEM

State and Local

As unwilling and as reluctant as it is, our public system of education represents the best resource for the development of a system of vocational guidance and vocational education to serve all youth and adults throughout the nation. In most states, the state and local investments in public education represent 50 percent or more of all expenditures. The very fact that the system exists is important. If we agree that we cannot afford a parallel educational system within this nation, then our effort must be to make massive changes in the educational system to meet the needs of our modern society, rather than to develop a competing and expensive new system under federal Manpower programs.

The public schools are funded in all states for at least a minimum level of operation and in some states are now reaching out to provide special services to parochial-school youth as well. Within our state, we are already providing some assistance to parochial schools in the area of instructional costs, busing, and special services. Judicious investments of funds into the public education system can be used as a method of bringing about changes in the curriculum and organization, providing that the persons administrating the funds at the federal, state and local level accept their responsibility for leadership as well as for money management.

I believe sincerely that such a conversion is possible. Our experiences in investing funds over the years in vocational education has proven to us that local school districts will more than match investments made from state and federal funds for that program. Our experiences in Ohio during the 1969–70 school year also lead us to believe that small investments of dollars into junior high school level programs and early high school programs, discussed later in this chapter, can be used to change the direction of curriculum and to reorient the attitudes and practices of the existing staff at those levels.

All the fault for lack of changes does not rest in the public school system itself, but often the reluctance to change is caused by the methods used to fund education at the federal, state and local levels. The public schools cannot do the job that we envision without added financial resources and without leadership from the state and national levels. More adequate funding is needed. A funding pattern must be developed which will assure changes in the system rather than a maintenance of status quo. To ignore the existence of our public school system as a major resource in the development of a system of vocational guidance and vocational education would be to move towards failure and bankruptcy.

The alternative to the improvement of our system of state and local public schools and the related parochial and private schools would be the establishment of a nationwide system of vocational education under the guise of Manpower Education. By whatever name it might be called, it would still be a federal system of education, and such a practice could in the future open the way to the minds of men on the part of an unscrupulous person or organization at the Washington level.

We must maintain a public education system independent of federal control. We need only to remember the fact that Hitler, through control of the education of youth, changed the face of Germany within the period of ten years. Proper investments through our public education system could be used in our nation to make massive progress in the solution of our social and economic problems if we became serious about the use of that system for solutions. Conversion of the system is not only possible, it is mandatory if we hope to continue as a free nation in a technological age.

Guidance Personnel

The number of vocational guidance education personnel in our state and throughout the nation established with financial assistance from the Vocational Education Amendments of 1968 and state funds is very small. Title V of the National Defense Education Act, however, which provided money to public schools to assist with a portion of the cost of the guidance counselors, stimulated the employment of more guidance counselors. The large number of trained professional guidance counselors existing in our state and in the nation could be a very positive force in the development of an adequate system of vocational guidance and vocational education. My contacts with this group would lead me to believe that they are an able and dedicated group of people and can become a very significant force in the total educational program if they were to accept a major responsibility for the development of a system of Vocational Guidance rather than a cult of guidance and counseling centered in the professional guidance counselor.

The vocational guidance system proposed in this book is curriculum-centered, not guidance counselor-centered. I would suggest, however, that the guidance counselor has both a leadership role and a supporting role in the programs that will be outlined, if he is willing to give up the concept that he is the guidance program.

The Governor's Task Force

The Governor's Task Force, mentioned earlier, which included representation from business, industry, education, and government, reported to me in January 1969 that we face a crisis in service to youth and that we must invoke an attitude of concern equal to the severity of the problem. The report indicated that during the 1968 school year the dropout rate from an inner-city school of a major city between September and December was 8.8 percent of the total enrollment. During that same period, the dropout rate of students enrolled in approved vocational education courses in the same school was only 1 percent. This and other data convinced the Task Force that students provided with a relevant education would stay in school. The Task Force suggested use of the following resources in encouraging a system of vocational guidance and vocational education:

1. A massive informational program should be conducted, utilizing all public media to present vocational and technical education as rewarding and worthy choices in education.

   The Governor of Ohio should continue leading in this area as should all other key personages in government and education. Positive facts concerning employment-oriented education should be presented.

2. Areas of responsibility for this program should be assigned.

   The State Superintendent of Public Instruction should organize all information programs calling for school district involvement. The Director of Development should enlist the support of leaders in business, commerce and industry. The Directors of Employment, Urban Affairs and Welfare should marshal their clients into available programs. Local education leaders should recruit business, commerce, labor, parental, social and educational interests at the county or sub-county level.

3. Leaders in the mass communication media must grasp the scope and nature of the crisis.

   Leaders in all related fields should funnel to the mass communications industry facts on every aspect of the problem. These state and community leaders should pose the problems and discuss solutions with reporters, editors and publishers. The recommendations contained in this report are the best ways the Task Force has found to solve the crisis, but they are not to be interpreted as exhaustive or exclusive.

4. Vocational education should be uniformly defined as skilled-job oriented.

   All leaders should know vocational education as a program to prepare students for meaningful employ-

ment and to give them some actual job experience before high school graduation.

5. Technical Education should be uniformly defined as college-level preparation.

All leaders should understand technical education as a
two-year college-level education that prepares students
to assist graduate professionals in many diverse fields
including medicine and engineering. Technical education should prepare for para-professional employment
and should offer an Associate Degree from a respected
university or college.

6. Potential students should be told the value of an employment-oriented education.

The Board of Regents reports that the graduates of
technical education programs are starting at salaries
ranging upwards from $6,000 a year.

The want ads in a major city's newspaper show that a
beginning welder with knowledge of the field and work
experience can expect to earn nearly $6,000 per year.
The International Brotherhood of Electrical Workers
reported any of its members, after apprenticeship, can
earn $12,000 in 1968, and because of contracts al-
ready signed, can expect to earn $17,000 in 1971
based on a 40-hour week.

For comparison, beginning instructors at universities
often earn below $6,000 a year, although the average
reported salary for a full professor at Ohio State University was $16,565 during the 1968-69 school year.
Facts comparable to these, compiled locally, can show
the economic value of an employment-oriented education.

7. Parents must learn to value employment-oriented education.

Leaders at all levels must assure parents that a college
degree in itself does not guarantee success or happiness. Success and happiness are relative, and mean different things to every individual. Employment at the
highest level of an individual's interest and ability is a
measure of success and inherently satisfying.[1]

The Task Force recommendations for a system of vocational guidance and vocational education serve as the backbone for the system
under development within our state:

---

[1] *A Report by the Governor's Task Force on Vocational and Technical Education* (State of Ohio, 1969).

First Six Grades
1. Respect for the world of work
2. Motivation to want to do some part of the world of work

Grades Seven and Eight
    Career orientation of all students to our technological society

Grades Nine and Ten
1. Exploration for occupational choice
2. Work adjustment program for school disoriented youth

Grades Eleven and Twelve (sixteen years of age and up)
    Broad, goal-centered educational programs

Post-High School
1. Technical education
2. Professional education
3. Retraining of unemployed and upgrading of employed workers

The National Panel of Consultants on Vocational Education, reporting to President Johnson in 1968, recognized the vital importance of vocational guidance to the nation and the effectiveness of vocational and technical education.[2] This panel, chaired by Dr. Martin Essex, State Superintendent of Public Instruction for Ohio, recommended that an adequate staff for vocational guidance be maintained in both the U.S. Office of Education and in State Departments of Education. The report of the panel indicated that vocational guidance was not sufficiently available to all youth and adults and recommended strongly that vocational guidance be made accessible to all. The panel stated, "Vocational guidance and vocational and technical education are interdependent, one needs the other. Each ceases to be effective if the other is left out. It is inadequate or is of poor quality." I believe one could state categorically that there can be a system of vocational education and vocational guidance only if all parts of the system are present and available to the youth throughout his educational career. There can be no system of vocational guidance without an adequate

---

[2] *Vocational Education, The Bridge between Man and His Work,* U.S. Dept. of Health, Education, and Welfare (Washington, D.C.: U.S. Government Printing Office, 1968).

program of vocational and technical education, and there cannot be an adequate program of vocational and technical education without an effective system of vocational guidance. The report of this panel served as the development of the Vocational Education Amendments of 1968, PL 90-576.

Research from the Federal Manpower Program

Another resource for the development of a system of vocational guidance and vocational education is the research and experiences resulting from the operation of various manpower programs organized under the Manpower Development and Training Act of 1963 and under the Office of Economic Opportunity for youth who have dropped out of school and for unemployed adults. I believe that it is a sad commentary that billions of dollars were spent by the Office of Economic Opportunity on the Job Corps Centers under contracts with industrial organizations in such a manner that the Centers provided little opportunity for the people responsible for our public schools to learn from their failures. The operation of the residential centers for dropouts could have taught the public schools how to better serve the youth and prevent dropouts.

I see absolutely no justification for any boy or girl under the age of 18 to be out of school and out of work. A public education system does not have the right to throw its rejects onto a labor market that has no work for these rejects. We must, however, give the public schools the financial assistance and research data to help them to establish programs which can be of significant service to all youth, including the youth who have previously voted against the present educational system by walking out of the public schools.

It is my observation, and evidently the observation of others, that the Job Corps Program as conceived and administered under the Office of Economic Opportunity was an expensive failure. The program costs per student have been reported as averaging in the neighborhood of $9,000. In some of the least successful Job Corps Centers, the cost reached $40,000 per individual student. Job Corps Centers are being re-oriented, but the new organization places them under the U.S. Department of Labor, with no direct liaison with the state and local people responsible for the education of our youth.

There is no evidence that in spite of massive per-pupil costs, the operation of the Job Corps Centers by agencies other than education was any more successful in working with the youth than were the public schools. I believe the public schools should be made to live with their mistakes, to learn from those mistakes, and to reorganize educational programs in such a way that they serve all youth and not only the college-bound. Within our own state, we identified the need for a residential center similar to the OEO Job Corps Centers, and established such a center at the Mahoning Valley Air Force Base with the assistance of funds from the Manpower Development and Training Act. This action was taken even before the Job Corps Centers were opened. This center was organized and operated through the cooperation of our Division of Vocational Education and Division of Vocational Rehabilitation in the State Department of Education and the Ohio State Employment Service, with the assistance of a non-profit corporation established by a grant from an industrialist concerned about the needs of youth. This center for disadvantaged youth, out of school and out of work, taught us much about the nature of these young people and about the failures of our present system of education.

We found, for instance, that almost none of the youth enrolled in the center had ever talked to a guidance counselor. Yet their interest in talking to a guidance counselor was such that we had to expand our original number of guidance counselors planned and make the guidance counselors available in the evening for conference because of the intense interest of the youth in this service.

We learned many things from the operation of the residential program at the Mahoning Valley Vocational School. We learned that youth who rejected school were willing to participate in an education program if we could show them that this program would help them get a job. The youth enrolled in this center could not be motivated by the concept, "You must take this hard course because it's good for you." They could, however, be motivated on the basis that, "If you learn this trade, you can earn a good living."

When we gave these dropouts an opportunity to prepare for a job, they no longer resisted education, including the education to read, write and figure.

We learned from our experiences at the Mahoning Valley Vocational Center that over half the dropouts referred to the center had something wrong with them physically or mentally which made it difficult or impossible for them to participate in the educational program without rehabilitation services. Through cooperation of the Division of Vocational Rehabilitation, such rehabilitation services were made a part of the total educational program. Living with these youths on a 24-hour day basis was a sobering experience. From Mahoning Valley we learned many lessons which are now being implemented into our present efforts in Vocational Guidance and Vocational Education within our state.

Perhaps such residential centers can be justified only if they will provide us with experiences and research data which will help us revise our present educational system so that the residential centers for disadvantaged youth will not be needed in the future. The residential centers are an expensive form of remediation which would not be needed if our system of education was relevant to the needs of all youth. Columnist Alice Widener, visiting the Mahoning Valley Vocational Center, had this to say:

> At the Mahoning Valley Vocational School near Youngstown, Ohio, there is now taking place a unique pioneering effort in vocational training for disadvantaged boys from 16 through 21 years of age.
>
> Set up at a phased-out Air Force base, the Mahoning School is operated by several state groups working together to solve the basic educational problem that led to hasty creation of the ill-fated Job Corps and similar poverty program activities.
>
> The school, a residential training place, is a really good example of how seed money from federal funds can be used effectively and profitably by local and state officials working with educators and industrial executives.
>
> During several hours conversation with more than 30 young men who were school dropouts and former delinquents in one way or another, I heard the kind of plain honest talk that explains more clearly than volumes of academic sociological studies exactly what these boys' problems are.

"I work better with my hands than my head," said a pale-faced blond boy. "Here at this school they don't put the pressure on you to be what you don't want to be and can't be. They don't look down on you for wanting to be what you want to be."

"All that business about kids being equal is for the birds," said a youth about to be graduated from the school, where he studied mechanical drawing; an industrial job is waiting for him.

"I learned more math here at the drawing board than I ever did in school where most of the kids always were ahead of me. I just can't think so fast. I couldn't keep up and the teacher just had to rush everybody along. My family is in a mess and school was my chance to get away from them and ahead. But tryin' to go ahead at regular school and not learnin' a trade was too much, just too much!"

Said a boy with an intelligent face showing new-found maturity: "Everybody was telling us that if we didn't make it through high school and to college we'd be on the junk heap. My folks took out insurance to send me to college. They said they were giving me a chance to get ahead and to do better than they did in life. Well, I've got a job waiting for me when I finish up here that'll pay me more than my old man is getting right now. I read better, write better, and talk better now and I like studying because I can see where it leads to."

Like all human endeavors, the present system at Mahoning School was arrived at by trial-and-error. Early mistakes are now corrected. I never saw a more self-respecting, disciplined, ambitious, and purposeful group of young men than the "disadvantaged" youths now in residence at Mahoning Vocational School. The pupil-teacher relationship is remarkably good.

It is not surprising that a veritable pilgrimage to Mahoning is taking place by officials in Federal and out-of-state welfare departments. Seventy-five percent of the so-called "problem" youths trained at Mahoning in courses lasting from six months to one year have found jobs and are keeping them.

"In vocational education," say Dr. Byrl R. Shoemaker, Director of Ohio vocational education, "we weave together the principles of math and science, skills and technical knowledge into a mix which will help youth and adults to enter and adjust to employment opportunities or to upgrade themselves in their chosen field of work."

We should adopt new attitudes toward vocational education.

A terrible disservice is being done to our youth today, in my judgment, by intellectual leaders, insurance and banking executives, government, and industrial leaders who keep on telling young people they are destined for poverty and inferiority unless they get a college degree.

Only 14 percent of young people become college graduates. Why not train the 86 percent so that they can answer the basic employment question: "What can you do?"

Today 60 percent of the American work force is in the service occupations. Why not train young people to fill and hold such jobs well and efficiently, always leaving the way open to advancement.

There always is "room at the top" for boys and girls determined to get there. But why neglect or mistreat educationally the vast majority filling the rungs of the ladder from bottom to top?[3]

National Vocational Education Acts

The Vocational Education Act of 1963, PL 88-210, and the Vocational Education Amendments of 1968, PL 90-576, both approved the use of vocational guidance programs. Traditionally, however, funds for the vocational guidance program have gone to purchase the services of guidance personnel to be identified normally as vocational guidance counselors. While these counselors have proven to be valuable, working in a direct relationship with the vocational programs in our public schools, the concept of guidance that I am encouraging in this book envisions the employment of the vocational guidance counselors as only one part of a total system of vocational guidance and vocational education. The Vocational Education Amendments of 1968 provided the first real breakthrough in funding which will encourage the development of the type of system that I envisioned.

For the first time in the history of federal vocational education acts, specific money was provided as a part of the Act for exemplary programs of a pre-vocational nature. For the first time, the Act

---

[3] *Columbus Dispatch,* February 2, 1967.

envisioned the development of a system starting with kindergarten and moving throughout the work life of the individual. While the term *pre-vocational education* was used to include programs such as vocational education in the elementary school, in reality these "pre-vocational" activities become guidance for choice rather than direct training for occupations. There is no question that the work habits, attitudes, concepts and relationships developed by a good system of vocational guidance also contribute to the success of the person in employment. The vocational guidance phase of the system would be characterized by activities leading to attitudes, understandings and choice, rather than to skills and technical knowledge relating to entrance into occupations.

One section of the Vocational Education Amendments of 1968, PL 90-576, states in part:

1. "planning and developing exemplary programs or projects; and
2. "establishing, operating, or evaluating exemplary programs or projects designed . . . to broaden occupational aspirations and opportunities for youths, with special emphasis given to youths who have academic, socioeconomic, or other handicaps."

    These programs or projects may, among others, include:
    (a) "those designed to familiarize elementary and secondary school students with the broad range of occupations for which special skills are required and the requisites for careers in such occupations;
    (b) "programs or projects for students providing educational experiences through work during the school year or in the summer; and
    (c) "programs or projects for intensive occupational guidance and counseling during the last years of school and for initial job placement."

    In addition, Federal funds for vocational guidance and counseling may be used in conducting:
1. "research in vocational education;
2. "training programs designed to familiarize persons involved in vocational education with research findings and successful pilot and demonstration projects in vocational education;

3. "experimental, developmental, and pilot programs and projects designed to test the effectiveness of research findings;
4. "demonstration and dissemination projects;
5. "the development of new vocational education curricula; and
6. "projects in the development of new careers."

The Vocational Education Amendments of 1968 also directed the expenditure of funds for the disadvantaged, handicapped and post-secondary education. Whether or not it was the intent of the Act, the goals of the Act and the provisions included in the Act could well provide for a revolution in the curriculum in grades kindergarten through 12. The changes in educational programming suggested by some of the provisions of the Act have nothing to do with the narrowly conceived college preparatory curriculum at the high school level or a junior high school system at grades 7, 8 and 9, mimicking the high school or a Dick-Jane-Spot concept in grades K through 6. The Vocational Education Amendments, 1968, do not impose any certain system upon the states, and I suppose it will be possible for states to ignore the plea for social and economic impacts made by the Act. The Act closely paralleled the concepts of the Governor's Task Force Report referred to earlier.

It is my earnest plea that programs initiated under assistance from the Vocational Education Amendments of 1968 envision a more comprehensive system than can be funded under the meager allowance made in the appropriations under the Act. It is true that neither the appropriations nor the authorization are adequate to achieve the goals established in the Act, but proper use of the funds made available for experimentation and demonstration could encourage the allocation of more monies to vocational education at both state and national levels. In the Act, there are over thirty references to possible funding of vocational guidance and counseling.

SUMMARY

The basic resources for the development of a system of Vocational Guidance and Vocational Education are present in our public education system. Yes, the system is antiquated and out of date. But it contains the physical facilities, staff, community relationships, and funding processes necessary for the development of such a system. We cannot afford to buy a new system of education. We must convert the one that we have.

The guidance personnel within that system represent a resource which can provide leadership and supplemental services to the development of a system of vocational guidance. They must, however, accept their place as a part of the system rather than the central core of a guidance and counseling program which places the emphasis upon individual counseling.

The need for a system of vocational guidance and vocational education was reported by a Governor's Task Force in the state of Ohio in January, 1969. This Task Force recommended an occupationally oriented program starting in kindergarten and continuing through the work life of the individual. The Task Force envisioned changes in the existing educational program as a means of achieving goals they identified by grade level.

We have gained some knowledge and insights into the needs of disadvantaged youths and adults through the Manpower Training Program when such programs are operated in cooperation with the public education system. We lost a massive opportunity for the re-direction of our educational system when the operation of the Job Corps Center was given to industry and business. The educational program in the public schools must be changed in such a manner that residential centers like the Job Corps would no longer be needed.

Perhaps one of the major resources for the development of the system of Vocational Guidance and Vocational Education proposed rests in the Vocational Education Amendments of 1968, which, in cooperation with state and local funds, can make investments into the educational system in such a manner that changes could be made through the use of existing staff and facilities rather than a totally new organization.

Chapter 5

VOCATIONAL GUIDANCE IN THE ELEMENTARY CURRICULUM

Curriculum-Centered Guidance

Schools have begun to employ guidance counselors at the elementary school level, but there is no indication that a system of vocational guidance is developing in grades kindergarten through 6 in any school district in the state—perhaps not in the nation.

The words *vocational* and *guidance* are used together, as in the National Vocational Guidance Association, but there is little emphasis on the vocational in guidance literature about programs or in guidelines for services in the elementary schools. Reference to guidance in the elementary schools still is counselor- and counseling-centered. While the services of a guidance counselor can be used effectively at the elementary level, the assumption seems to be that if there is no counselor, no guidance will take place. In the absence of a guidance counselor, vocational guidance takes place indirectly, for better or worse, through the teachers and others. Perhaps worse than no guidance counselor is a counselor in the elementary school without an accompanying system of vocational guidance.

The youth in the elementary grades are very impressionistic and are gathering concepts and ideas through their contacts with their parents and their teachers which will affect them throughout their lifetime. The parent who says, "I don't want you to work as hard as I have, I want you to go to college and be something," and the teachers who threaten youth with the fact that they will have to "work" throughout their lifetime unless they do their lessons well forget that professions involve work and that they are having a greater guidance impact on the young person than any factual presentation made later by a guidance counselor, no matter how well-trained or -educated he may be.

Yes, we need educational guidance and personal guidance in the elementary grades. But we also need a vocational guidance program at the core of the system for guidance in the elementary school.

Goals for the Elementary Level

I would suggest two goals (identified in previous chapters) for the system of vocational guidance in the elementary curriculum:

1) To develop in all youth respect for all work
2) To motivate all youth to want to take their place in the world of work

These two concepts read so simply that I ask you to read them again and think about them. They might well become the core of the educational curriculum in the elementary school around which the rest of the curriculum would be built.

In fulfilling the first goal, a vocational guidance system in the elementary school can keep a young person from seriously limiting his scope of occupational choice by a snobbish attitude towards many types of work. I do not propose or believe that youth should make an occupational choice at the end of elementary school. My concern is that he develop the necessary attitudes toward work so his later decisions will be made with an open mind. All work is honorable, and every man or woman is worthy of respect if they do their job well. A Task Force on Vocational-Technical Education, established in one of the major cities, arrived at conclusions which supported the need to prepare youth for work. One of the important conclusions of this task force was as follows:

> Exploration of the world of work ought to begin at kindergarten level, and as an integrated part of the curriculum through all grade levels. Give each student a realistic concept of the actual content of all levels of occupations from unskilled jobs to semi-skilled and skilled craft levels, technical and service occupations, business and clerical occupations, through the professions. Much greater use should be made of field trips and resource persons. This program should be conducted without prejudiced opinions or value judgements as to the relative worth or importance of the various ways our citizens make their contributions to society. Respect for all honest work ought to be the theme of this program.[1]

The second goal emphasizes "do something" rather than "be somebody." The "be somebody" complex is the one that causes parents to force their children into unwise decisions based upon status considerations; the "be somebody" complex tends to identify with the doctor-lawyer-merchant-chief positions providing social status to the individual and his parents. Has our obsession with the socially acceptable professions reduced all other occupations to a level of menial tasks and stripped these important jobs of the pride of achievement that went with such work? People in New York City soon found how important the garbage and trash collection was to the entire city when the collections stopped for a short time. People who accept welfare as a way of life lose the satisfaction that can come only with achievement through work. Work in itself is a

---

[1] "Report of Task Force on Vocational Education," *Journal of Program Research and Development,* Cincinnati Public Schools, Vol. IV, No. 3 (June, 1969).

means of earning a living, earning self-respect and respect of others, and a self-discipline necessary for effective citizenship in our form of government.

I wonder what massive change might be wrought if in the first six years of school all youth were to accept the two basic concepts listed above.

PILOT PROGRAMS IN OHIO

It is the goal of Ohio's Division of Vocational Education and Division of Guidance and Testing in the State Department of Education to initiate in the fall of 1970 pilot systems of vocational guidance in 15 elementary schools of various sizes and social economic status. The pilot schools will represent a cross section of the type and size of school districts within our state. Due to the serious nature of the problems in our major cities, most of the pilot centers selected will be from the eight major cities in our state. Small city systems and rural educational centers will be included, however, in order to determine the effectiveness of the effort in a number of different situations.

Schools selected must agree to establish a system in Kindergarten through Sixth Grade and must agree to serve all youth through the system, rather than a selected few. In selection of the pilot centers, attention will be given also to the economic level within such centers in order to determine if such a system is as important in an affluent area as it would be in an inner-city section of one of our major cities.

Roles of the School Personnel

The plan under consideration started with the involvement of the principals and teachers in order to insure the fact that the program will be curriculum-centered rather than centered around the individual. Professionals in the guidance field were a part of the planning unit and participated in a system developed. The elementary curriculum, however, must be the basis for the establishment of the system if it is to be successful. This concept goes back to the position stated earlier in this book that the curriculum must be utilized in order for the program to affect all youth. The curriculum is the basis for the vocational guidance system proposed, and the leadership for the planning and the implementation of the system must be the elementary principals and teachers.

While other professionals, particularly the professional guidance counselor, can have an input into the program, the leadership role must be that of the elementary principal and the implementation role must be that of the elementary teacher.

The development of a vocational guidance system in the elementary school must start with the re-orientation of the staff of that school. They must be encouraged to accept a coupling of knowledge with practice which does not in any way lessen the importance of the skill subjects, but gives them greater meaning in the welding of theory and facts. This is not at all a new concept, but merely returns to the concept of the early theoreticians in education: the world of school and the world of work must be made one world. Students need to learn that every job requires some type of preparation, either formal education, or on-the-job apprenticeship, that their work skills must be updated as occupations change, that at times new jobs must be learned as occupations are dropped, that most jobs will require training prior to entry. They must also learn to understand themselves and the need to develop their abilities and interests. Curriculum is the basis for the development of these fundamental concepts; the principals and the teachers are responsible for organizing and implementing the curriculum.

Organization and Implementation

Statewide planning for the implementation of the vocational guidance system in elementary schools should involve a committee combining professional educators and lay people. State departments of education must provide initial leadership. The massive needs for changes in improvements in the educational system cannot await the very slow, evolutionary process of change of growing from community to community on the basis of example and observation. State Departments of Education must take a leadership role.

The statewide planning committee should include representation from the state P.T.A. organization, state advisory council for vocational education, principals of some of the elementary schools considered in the project, teachers from elementary schools, state legislature, guidance profession and division of vocational education within state departments. The guidance profession should be well-represented by people from the state level of administration in the Division of Guidance and from university guidance departments. Emphasis in selection of the personnel should be upon people who are responsible for making things happen, rather than upon theoreticians who can withdraw and retreat to safe ground when there is work to be done or problems to be faced. The state committee for action should identify concept goals in keeping with the broad goals identified earlier in this chapter, alternative processes that can be utilized to implement these goals, and the types of materials and additional services necessary in schools implementing the program which would require additional funds.

No school should be chosen for participation in the pilot programs in which the principal of that school is not fully in agreement with the need for such a program and willing to work cooperatively with the teachers to bring about such program developments. *The principal is the key figure,* much more important than any other outside resource personnel that may be made available. The teachers are a close second in importance to the principal, but without the support of the principal, the hodge-podge of teacher effort will be somewhat less than effective. The committee may choose to employ vocational guidance counselors, consultants and resource persons on a continuing basis in the projects. A vocational guidance counselor could provide the liaison relationships between the school and the community to organize field trips out of the school and to bring resource people into the school. Perhaps the vocational education personnel can best serve to determine whether the program focuses upon work and the curriculum includes the kinds of experiences which will develop the concepts toward which the program is directed. Vocational education personnel would also have access to materials planned for vocational education which might be of assistance to the teachers and principals developing the materials for the program. Vocational educators also have contacts with industry and business, and industry and business must be involved to make the program successful.

At the local levels, school advisory councils, involving parents, teachers and possibly some pupils, should be established for those schools who participate in the program. Within the local school, concepts need to be developed by grade level in keeping with the general concepts established by the statewide committee. Processes which draw upon experience-based efforts in utilizing concepts of the core curriculum identified in an earlier chapter, in which subject line areas or divisions are ignored or made less divisive, must be developed in order to achieve the concept development at each grade level. It must be a system, not a single sporadic effort in one grade or at one time in the school year.

The responsibility for the programming and the implementation must be shared with the community through the involvement of the community as a resource for experiences or simulated experiences. The program must have both human and material resources needed to meet the goals. Curriculum units must be developed which will fit the specifications of the goals and directed at age and grade level of the students involved. These curriculum units should outline the *behavior to be achieved* and *methods of achieving the behavior*. The curriculum packets should involve not only instructional material, but should indicate different methods of implementing the instructional program through such techniques as simulation or role playing. This approach will be a learning process for the guidance counselors as well as for the teachers and principals.

Developing a Proposal for a World of Work Program

Guidelines have been developed by the Ohio Division of Vocational Education for the establishment of World of Work programs in kindergarten through grade 6. Priority is to be given to those school systems that have developed career orientation programs at grades 7 and 8.

The guidelines were developed by a committee including elementary principals, guidance counselors, counselor educators, vocational educators and others.

The guidelines are brief and flexible, but follow the concept of changing the existing curriculum and of utilizing existing staff. The guidelines forwarded to the schools were as follows:

I.   *Purposes and Need for a World of Work Education Program at the Elementary Level*

Most students enrolled in present day elementary education programs have little opportunity to become acquainted with the world of work and realize how learning to read and write and use mathematics has any relationship to a future job or career. The purpose of this program is to insert into the K-6 curriculum a procedure whereby every student will gain the experiences and exposure to the world of work which will enable him to see how education leads toward jobs and careers. It should further help each student to have a better understanding of work as a part of life and its importance in our technological society. This will provide students also with an understanding of the wide spectrum of jobs and careers that are really available and help them to gain a respect for opportunities to earn a living. It is not intended that this program will prepare youngsters for any sort of a job nor will it require them to make a decision as to what in which career they are interested. It simply should provide a re-organized approach to elementary education which will cause students to be more aware of the wide range of occupational opportunities available to them. A secondary value of a program of this type would be the involvement of the community as a part of the school program to help prevent the alienation and separation of school from life. Hopefully the program of this type would result in better and more effective education in the academic sense through increased student interest and motivation.

II.   *Preparation and Submission of a Proposal*

1. Any local public board of education may prepare and submit a proposal.
2. In order for a proposal to be considered for funding during FY 1971, it must be submitted to the Division of Vocational Education.

3. Proposals must include a complete description of the operation of the program in terms of the minimum requirements for consideration as listed below.

4. Proposals will be reviewed by a review panel made up of persons knowledgeable concerning elementary education and the world of work.

III. *Minimum Requirements to be Met by Proposals*

1. Proposals must make provision for including all students, grades K-6, in the program. If only one or two school buildings in a district are included, then all of the students in any one of those buildings that is included in the proposal must be involved in the program. It is not the intent of this project to develop a program that only serves certain kinds or types of youngsters.

2. The proposal must include a detailed description and scheduling of the activities and experiences provided to the students at all grade levels, K-6. The schedule developed could be offered in blocks of time or units of time integrated throughout the K-6 curriculum. Emphasis should be placed on including student activities and experiences that relate to the world of work, such as the use of tools, equipment, and materials within the classroom to provide an activity-oriented approach to learning about jobs, excursions and field trips, interviews with parents and other people who work for a living as a part of the classroom activity, forming companies and actually producing a small product such as paperweight or cookies, etc., to learn the operation of business. Individual and group activities planned with definite responsibilities for students; such activities related to real jobs and careers, etc.

3. Proposals must show a curriculum, K-6, that has regularly scheduled a minimum of 270 hours per year of world of work activity experiences in grades 1-6 and a minimum of 135 hours per year in kindergarten. These activities and experiences could be arranged at the discretion of the local system. In some cases large blocks of time might be utilized, in other cases integrated short periods of activity could be included within the curricular areas.

4. Local Advisory Committee must be used in building the proposal. This committe should include representatives from the following groups:

     1. Parents
     2. Teachers
     3. Other community groups

  5. Program evaluation procedures must be developed as part of the proposal. The evaluation plan should provide for on-going as well as final end-of-year evaluation.

IV. *Reimbursement of Approved Programs of Elementary Education, World of Work*

  1. Reimbursement for approved programs of elementary education, world of work will be made at the end of each fiscal year and pursuant to the submission of the appropriate approvable affidavits and evaluation reports.

  2. A budget breakdown must be included as a part of the project proposal.

  3. Approved programs of elementary education, world of work will be reimbursed at the rate of $15.00 for each student, enrolled K-6.

SUMMARY

Two broad goals are suggested as the basis for the vocational guidance impact in the elementary curriculum. These become the broad concepts about which the program would be developed.

The program is not to be counselor-centered, but curriculum-centered, with experience as the basis of the curriculum. If a curriculum-centered project is to succeed, the principals and teachers of the elementary schools involved must accept the leadership role in the program. The curriculum project developed in relationship to these broad goals should not be inserted into the curriculum, taught for a short period of time one year or each year, but should permeate the curriculum. The impact of the proposed program would carry over into the total educational program provided in the elementary school in terms of the reading, writing and arithmetic. Successful curriculum must have experience at the core—experience in terms of simulation, observation, participation, role-playing. Written and visual instructional materials or aids should be supplementary to such experiences, not the sole means of experience.

The guidance counselor and the vocational educator are important to the functioning of this vocational guidance system in the elementary school, but in a supplementary and supporting role rather than in the leadership role. Leadership for the initiation of the program on a statewide basis, however, might well emanate from the divisions of vocational education and guidance and testing within the state departments of education in the various states.

Such a program, correctly implemented, would serve as a stimulus to the student throughout the remainder of his public school career as an encouragement for making an occupational choice at a later date and as a basis for development of self-respect in whatever occupation he will serve as an adult. Such a program will take an investment of state and/or federal dollars in addition to the funds presently made available for the elementary school curriculum, but the investment of money, if it is made a part of the existing curriculum in the elementary school, will not be as great as attempting to develop a totally new supportive program tacked on to the elementary school. I am suggesting a redirection of resources presently available in the public schools, rather than a massive addition of personnel to do a job that the school should be doing. As I indicated, there will be additional costs, but not nearly the costs of reproducing a second educational system or correcting the deficiencies of graduates of the present system.

Chapter 6   A CAREER ORIENTATION PROGRAM FOR GRADES SEVEN AND EIGHT, AGES 12 AND 13

Purpose

There is a very simple fact that is grossly ignored within our nation. Our economy is a profit system. Too often profit has been sneered at as an evil. Rather, it should be respected as the backbone of our economic system.

The profit system must mean profit to both the employer and the employee. To the employer the profit means not only a return on his investment, but also a means providing for growth of his industry or business through research or through construction and equipment. The jobs that we need for an expanding economy and an expanding population must come from profits: no profit, no expansion. Likewise, each time the individual is paid for his work and his pay allows him to purchase more than the bare minimum of food and shelter, that also is profit, and from the expenditure of such profit by the individual the flow of goods and services enables the industrialist or businessman to expand his productive capabilities in order to provide for more jobs.

It is the sad truth that youth graduating from high schools or even from colleges fail to understand this simple economic fact. We have publicized in our state that profit is not a dirty word. Ohio is No. 1 in industrial growth. Our state administration also wants to publicize to the people of our state and to the industries and businesses of the nation that work is not a dirty word in Ohio, either.

The technological age in which we live is a much more complicated way of life than that into which we entered as youth. If we are successful in developing within the youth in the elementary school a respect for work and a motivation to work, then in junior high we must be ready to give an overview of the inter-relationships of our technological society. Youth at grades seven and eight, or ages 12 and 13, are beginning to look out at the world around them, beyond the confines of their individual family and friends. They have a great curiosity, a desire to know and learn, if only we will not dampen this desire to learn with a framework of cold and irrelevant, discipline-centered subjects.

Most youth of ages 12 and 13 are not ready to make occupational choices, although some youth have a burning desire for a certain occupational goal from early childhood on. I am not suggesting that those youth who have developed specific interests should be discouraged from such interests, since many of the men who have made great contributions in our world did so because of an interest which started early in youth. Rather I am suggesting that additional *experiences* be organized in grades seven and eight to provide all youth with an understanding of our technological society and the broad number of opportunities for earning a living as a part of that society. I am suggesting experience without forced choice for all youth.

Career Orientation as
Curriculum-Centered Guidance

The suggestion is made here that all youth of 12 and 13 years of age should be provided with an orientation to the careers possible in our technological society. In a career orientation program it is hoped that through student-centered activities the student will be exposed to a large range of jobs and careers.

Traditional forms of our educational system usually teach disciplines separately. A discipline is presented for the sake of the skills contained within it; the relationship of one discipline to the other is ignored.

Our entire system resembles the structure of a tier cake— elementary school, junior high school, college, all touching each other, but never mixing or relating. This structure, and achievement in the disciplines is often irrelevant to the student's career goals and aims. The interest and concerns of the individual must be the center of all academic, scientific or career development. Much of the enchantment of the "why" of learning for the middle school youth is segmented with little or no relevance to the youth's career goal or ambitions. The wider goal and concern should be to show the student the relationship and interdependence of occupations and disciplines.

The career orientation concept has been introduced in Ohio into 15 pilot and demonstration centers to relate to the middle school youth the work opportunities in the wonderful but awesome technical world in which we live. The exposure of students to our economy will broaden the student's knowledge of the world of occupations and encourage him to begin to find himself in that world.

A program of career orientation should be more than compartmentalization of occupations. Compartmentalization thus far has always meant that occupations were taught either by a guidance counselor or the industrial arts teacher. Occasionally, when it seemed "appropriate," other disciplines would present career information when it could be related to the subject under discussion. In many of these instances only glamorous occupations were given attention. Students were not actually exposed to jobs or to a group of jobs. Job exposure was minimal or only related to a few professional, industrial or business careers.

This particular method limited the broadening of the student's understanding of job goals and encouraged job status considerations.

To re-orient our educational system to the needs of youth, our traditional program of education must be altered, and become more relevant to the world of work. Our schools must offer an integrated program with the orientation of students to the modern technological world as a central core.

The purpose of the career orientation program should be to provide students:

1. more adequate knowledge of a technological society and the jobs and career alternatives available.
2. a knowledge of the kind of education or training required and work traits necessary in obtaining employment and gaining success in jobs and careers.
3. a self-appraisal of personal skills, abilities and life aspirations.
4. an opportunity to develop attitudes toward the world of work which enables one to fulfill his job career goal.
5. an opportunity to develop an attitude that socially useful work has dignity and worth, and is necessary as a part of an integrated social economic system.

To make the career orientation program cover the widest range of the society in which we live, a program must permeate the entire school. The exposure cannot be treated as an isolated subject, but as a central theme or core in the curriculum that contributes to the entire motivation and enrichment of the many areas of experience necessary for the growth and development of the students. There should not be a career orientation program teacher trained specifically for that task. Instead, as in the program for the elementary school, the principal and the teachers presently employed to serve the Seventh and Eighth Grades become the key personnel and the leaders for the introduction of career orientation into the school program. The orientation program should be incorporated within the school curriculum and taught as a part of the schedule of the regular teachers in the school. As an example, the industrial arts teachers could handle the area of construction and manufacturing. The mathematics teachers could handle the business careers. The social studies teacher could handle service careers and jobs ranging all the way from police and fire department personnel to government employees and hospital workers, including physicians. The scope of the career orientation program should cover such broad areas as manufacturing, construction, agriculture, health, service, business, communications, transportations, sales and marketing. Each of the major areas of employment would include all levels of jobs. For example, in the construction and manufacturing area, opportunities for employment ranging from the laborer to the professional engineer would be included.

Within the pilot programs in Ohio the career orientation programs are implemented in several ways, depending upon the construction of the school's curriculum. The primary methods of implementation follow three patterns. The first program of implementation is developed so that the career orientation is presented in regularly scheduled periods, coordinated and in an integrated form each day by all teachers throughout the year. Involvement of all the disciplines would present occupational information and student experiences as they related to the subject matter. The graphic matrix of Figure 6-1 illustrates this method.

In the illustration of this matrix, a discipline presents a relevance with many different areas of occupations and industries.

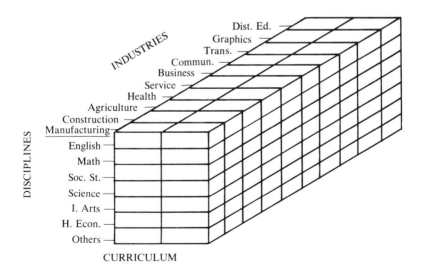

FIGURE 6–1

Each curriculum block is taught by teachers of the various disciplines. The teacher schedules the introduction of careers to coincide with presented subject matter, emphasizing the relationship of the subject matter to various jobs and careers.

The second plan for the implementation of career orientation programs provides career exposure at a concentrated period or periods during the year. This may take the form of presentation or activities to coincide with the intervals of the grading periods, thus presenting career exposure three, or possibly four times per year, depending upon the school's grading periods.

McTigue Jr. High School in Toledo, Ohio, on the tri-mester plan, has organized its career orientation program so that for two full weeks at the end of each tri-mester (six full weeks per year) all teachers, including coaches, music teachers, guidance personnel and regular teachers, spend all day on career orientation. Each teacher has a certain group of jobs and careers for which he is responsible. This teaching includes extensive use of resource personnel and field trips as well as the use of instructional materials, filmstrips and other career-oriented media.

The first week of the two-week block at the end of each tri-mester is devoted to class discussion, study groups, projects, displays, orientation and jobs related to study areas. The second week of the two-week period includes parent involvement as resource persons in representing a broad range of occupations.

Resource persons are invited into the schools from business, industry and service occupations. Field experiences are scheduled throughout the two-week period, with field trips being planned to cover a total of approximately 200 different jobs, careers and professions. The planning for field trips and resource personnel are concentrated during each of the three two-week blocks at the end of the tri-mesters. In this particular plan, close program coordination and organization is cardinal and the involvement of the total school staff is insured.

Analysis of the first two-week orientation experience indicated that field trip experiences had been provided to 75 different businesses and industries in the Toledo area, and that 173 persons or companies supplied speakers and/or panels to talk with students.

The brief evaluation presented by the school by this first effort is as follows:

Comments from Speakers

All of the speakers felt that the program was a tremendous success and an extremely important aspect of student preparation. The vast majority of them said they would like to participate in the program in April. Several speakers indicated the need for assistance from us in preparing their presentations.

Community Reaction

Since the community was not polled, we can only go on the reactions received from the 134 parents who participated in the program and those who chose to respond on their own. The reaction of these people was overwhelmingly positive and complimentary for our efforts in this new and difficult task.

Student Reaction

For the most part, the students reflected the attitudes of their teachers. Teachers who worked to build a positive attitude usually got it. Teachers who had under-planned, or who were not in complete support of the program, found their students reflected this attitude.

Some Career Week Statistics

Pieces of literature available	1,559
Feet of film shown	24,400
Number of speakers	269
Number of field trips	128
Number of phone calls made	538
Hours of bus transportation	592¾
Number of miles driven	3,095
Number of Parents Involved	134
Number of Students Involved	1,260
Number of Teachers Involved	52
Number of Staff Members Involved	10

Teacher Comments and Recommendations on Pre-planning Week

(a) Pre-planning week could be shortened, since some teachers feel more adequate in planning for the next program.

(b) Some teachers failed to utilize the planning week to develop enough student-centered in-class activities.

(c) There was noted a definite need for more resource help for individual teacher programs.

Teacher Comments and Recommendations on Speakers

(a) Some speakers spoke too long and need to direct their talks to the subject of careers.

(b) Speakers should be prepared for the type of group that they will be speaking to.

(c) Teachers could use a brief resume of the speaker in order to prepare their classes.

(d) Handouts and/or visual presentations proved to be most successful with the majority of students.

Teacher Comments and Recommendations on Field Trips

(a) More field trips are needed for the lower ability groups.

(b) Careers rather than facilities need to be accented on tours.

(c) More variety is needed in some areas where subject area restricts their future.

(d) Attempts should be made to control the size of the groups.

Teacher Comments and Recommendations on Format

(a) A week of pre-planning and week of career orientation was too long.

(b) Schedule was too hectic; some teachers would like more free time to work with students in the classroom.

(c) A maximum of two speakers or activities should be planned for one day (Some areas had three).

(d) Some teachers needed unshared classroom space to work with their students.

(e) Avoid the use of the bleachers in the gym.

It is very possible that this approach of total staff involvement in a concentrated period of time may not only prove to be a very significant way to provide for career orientation for students, but an excellent way to affect the attitudes and understandings of the teachers.

A third alternate plan for a career orientation program is a combination of the two previously mentioned methods. Selected persons present certain aspects of career orientation information continuously in regularly scheduled sessions throughout the year until the intervals of grading period. At the intervals of grading periods, determined by the administration, the entire faculty would involve themselves in active participation in regularly scheduled exposure of students to jobs and careers, through field trips and other means.

The key concepts in a career orientation program are investment and involvement. An effective career orientation program cannot be hung on to an existing seventh and eighth grade curriculum. The curriculum must be revised to accept career orientation as an integral and central part of that curriculum. It is not possible to implement the concept of career orientation programs described above and continue to do all the things now done at the seventh and eighth grade level. No school system should attempt to implement the type of educational program described here unless they are willing to make radical adjustment of the curriculum organization.

Supplemental Assistance Needed

Since the existing faculty of the school is used, there is no necessity to hire a new faculty. Planning, however, indicated the need for financial assistance in order to make the program effective. A new pattern of financial assistance was developed for this pilot program effort based not on people's salaries, but upon program needs. A maximum figure of $9000 was established for an investment in each 200 students in the seventh and eighth grades.

The schools participating in the program then identified to the Division of Vocational Education the purposes for which the monies would be used. Funds can be used for in-service training, instructional materials, student transportation, leadership, personnel or for any activity related directly to the success of the career orientation program. Funds made available may not be put into the general fund to assist with already on-going costs in the schools. Funding is organized into such a pattern that future sessions of the state legislature can consider incorporating the cost of the program as a part of the state foundation program.

Funds under the Vocational Education Amendments of 1968 provide only enough money to assist with the organization of pilot programs in such areas as the career orientation programs identified here. If such programs are to serve all youth, then state allocations, under whatever type of foundation program is used in a state to provide assistance to local communities, must provide a type of increment to encourage school districts to initiate such a career orientation program. The state assistance must fund a part of the *additional costs* of the program to the local school district. Additional monies provided to local communities for such a project represents an investment in innovative programming, in a change in curriculum, if the school district is required to establish and operate such a program as a condition for getting the additional monies.

Any plan for financing the system of vocational guidance and vocational education must have a sound basis for continuing financial assistance at the level which would enable any worthwhile activity to be made available, not only to a pilot group of schools but to all youth who need such instruction throughout the state. I realize that this is the concept of categorical aid rather than a concept of general aid in which the school systems use the money provided as they please. I believe, however, that categorical aid will be essential in order to assure the type of changes necessary in the educational programs.

Implementation

The state and local involvement encouraged for the vocational guidance system at the elementary level (Chapter 5) was essentially the procedure followed in initiating the career orientation program within the State of Ohio. At the state level, a committee was established, involving representation from the Divisions of Vocational Education, Guidance and Testing and Elementary and Secondary Education within the State Department of Education, and teachers and principals from the junior high schools who volunteered to participate in this pilot program.

A career orientation program is operated by the local school administrator in cooperation with his total staff. The key to the success of the program is the principal; his leadership in helping the total teaching staff to plan and develop curriculum is vital to the program's success. After first involving his teachers, the local administrator brings in the vocational guidance personnel in the planning of the total curriculum. He also may assign a coordinator for the project. Local planners include parent groups and business and industrial representatives. They work with the local administrator and his staff in preparing a proposal that meets the state requirements.

One state requirement is that a minimum of 540 hours of regularly scheduled career orientation curriculum activities be provided over a two-year period. This means that each seventh and eighth grade student during his two years in those grades would receive a minimum of 540 hours of career exposure. It also means that all seventh and eighth grade students would have an opportunity to learn about all job and careers, regardless of whether they were going to be skilled craftsmen or professional persons. The objective is not that they should make a commitment in terms of selecting a career, but that they have an exposure to as wide a range of opportunity as possible, so that later they may be able to have a better base upon which to make a selection.

A vital component of program development is the involvement of the total teaching staff in an in-service education activity. The schools that are approved for programs need to conduct teacher in-service workshops in July and August so that adequate time is available for reorganization of the curriculum and the development of the program. The local schools are encouraged to use their staff and other community personnel in the development of materials. Resources of existing vocational education instructional materials laboratories are made available to local schools in preparing materials. Vocational teacher educator services are available to local school staffs as they conduct in-service workshops.

School staffs, including teachers, guidance counselors and administrators in the participating pilot schools have been eager to develop the career orientation curriculum. They have used this as an opportunity to help reorganize a total curriculum so that it becomes more relevant and meaningful to youth by centering it around jobs and careers.

The Division of Vocational Education is working with all the pilot schools to develop instructional materials which can be reproduced and made available to all of the participating school districts. A development of instructional units which can be used in various ways by different school systems is essential not only to the success of the existing pilot programs but also to the development of new programs throughout the state. The Division of Vocational Education becomes the focal point for the exchange of ideas and materials between the pilot centers.

Suggested guidelines have been developed for the approval of programs. The following guidelines were developed by the statewide committee and will be reviewed and revised after this first year of experience with the career orientation.

REQUIREMENTS FOR CAREER
ORIENTATION PROGRAM APPROVAL

The following requirements are suggested for approval of career orientation program proposals. Approvals will be in form of career orientation units.

A. Preparation of a written plan for program development, implementation and administration which includes an explanation of how the program will provide students with observational and activity-centered experiences relative to the world of work.

B. Submission of a formal application, accompanied by the program plan including the school class schedule with the career orientation curriculum blocks, to the Division of Vocational Education, State Department of Education.

C. Submission of a Career Orientation Program time-allotment schedule.

D. A minimum of 200 students (seventh and eighth grade) shall be required per unit approved.

E. The submission of a planned budget justifying the use of reimbursement for the unit.

Suggested Reimbursement (pattern) per Career Orientation Unit
An approved career orientation unit will be reimbursed
from state and federal funds at the rate of $9,000 annually.*

REQUIREMENT FOR CURRICULUM PLANNING

For example a school would arrange for a significant
block of time devoted to the curriculum blocks in the seventh
and eighth grade. At least 45 or more clock hours would be
devoted to each career orientation curriculum block area.
Provisions would be made for regularly scheduled curriculum
blocks that would include student activities and experiences
related to understanding job opportunities in:

Agriculture	Services:
Business	1. Personal Service
Construction and Manufacturing	2. Repair Service
Distribution and Marketing	Transportation

It will be noted that the Standard Industrial Classifica-
tion is broken into groups. It is recommended that all levels
of employment, i.e., skilled, managerial, technical, and professional, be included as a part of each group.

Emphasis should be placed upon using resource people
from agriculture, business and industry, as a means of helping
students learn about career opportunities. Numerous field trips
to observe jobs should be planned. The real world of work
should serve as the laboratory for orientation to careers.

Each of these suggested curriculum block areas would
be scheduled so that the students would be in all areas some-
time during these seventh and eighth grade years.

The career orientation curriculum blocks would be
taught by teachers in existing curriculum areas. For example; industrial arts would handle construction and manufacturing. Science could implement the professions and agriculture. Social studies could handle the service areas, math,
the business jobs, etc.

Note: When Vocational Education facilities and programs are available, they should be utilized in the orientation program. Industrial arts, social studies, science areas
and others can offer curriculum blocks.

---

* Revised for FY 1971 to $7,000 for new programs and $5,000 for continuing
programs.

It should be pointed out that all students would be in each of the curriculum blocks. Each curriculum block would be organized and regularly scheduled so that each student would receive a minimum of 540 hours in the career orientation curriculum during their two years in the seventh and eighth grade. Some schools may elect to schedule two periods each day, others may arrange for larger blocks of time interspersed throughout the year. Students could also be scheduled for orientation, to testing, occupational information, and other student development activities related to career orientation.

SUMMARY

Choosing a vocation is more difficult for today's young people than it has been for any other generation. There are thousands of different jobs and careers from which to choose, but our analysis of these jobs would point out that about 90 percent of the jobs available fit into about 240 job families. In the traditional programs of our educational institutions today the student has no opportunity to get a personal acquaintance with more than one or two jobs, if indeed he has that opportunity. The child of today rarely has a first-hand opportunity to observe the industrial processes which produce the products of our society. These processes and products are the foundation of the wealth and technological development of our country. The rapid development of this technology, the increase of occupational specialization, and the development of man's interdependence socially, economically, and vocationally, have created a need for vocational guidance. The program of career orientation described in this chapter is curriculum-centered, is planned for all students, requires the leadership of the principals of the schools and the teachers of the seventh and eighth grades in reorganizing the present school system rather than investing in a new school system, and provides the second block in our system of vocational guidance and vocational education.

It is not the intent of this program to force the student into an occupational choice at the end of the eighth grade, but to give him some concepts of self and some concepts of the world of work to lead him to the next building block in the system. This part of the system, growing out of the master plan suggested by a Governor's Task Force in Ohio, described in an earlier chapter, was the first phase of the vocational guidance part of the system implemented within the State of Ohio. Additional materials must be developed, techniques improved and revisions made in the plans on the basis of experience. It is being piloted in such a manner, however, that if successful, there will not be a need for a massive research allocation to be made to every junior high school in order to implement the program. The program is being developed so that it can be made a part of the total program of education, including procedures for financing that system of education.

There is nothing sacred in the present educational curriculum. I find little in the research concerning the curriculum which tells me that parts of it should not be junked in favor of the type of experience proposed here. I would emphasize again that in this discussion we are talking about serving all students in the educational curriculum, not just the intellectually gifted or the educationally mentally retarded. There is a place in our technological work world for all of the people if they are given the opportunity to prepare for that place. Dr. Martin Essex, our State Superintendent of Public Instruction, once made the statement, "Education is the most phenomenal development in the history of man—man's greatest boon. It undergirds representative government and individual opportunity. To sustain an affluent society it must be related to the American Dream of opportunity." We should plead with the educators to redirect the present education system in order to relate it to the American Dream of opportunity in the type of society in which we live and *will* live, not the society of our childhood or that of our fathers.

Chapter 7

A PROGRAM OF EXPLORATION FOR GRADES NINE AND TEN, AGES 14 AND 15

Need for Exploratory Program

The present high school program is a relic of pre-Civil War vintage existing in a modern technological age. The high school was born in the 1850's as a means of preparing people to enter the colleges to pursue the true professions of law, religion and medicine, and it was the unusual student who completed high school, rather than the normal run of students. Attendance in high school was a privilege, limited to the few. A committee of ten in 1893 consummated this wedding of high school and college through the development of the Carnegie units, pointing up the proper procedures for obtaining the credits to enter college. The discipline-centered studies imposed upon the high school curriculum by this college relationship has never had a basis in educational theory, but it certainly has been maintained as a predominant practice in our public schools. The group of ultra-academicians who worry about the growth of vocational education in our public schools have no qualms about the introduction of meaningless nonsense-symbol college preparatory subjects at the ninth grade. Such subjects do little more than measure the intelligence of the individual and ignore completely the principles of learning which indicate that for learning to be meaningful it must be experience-centered. This discipline-centered practice is even carried over into the very important area of instruction for participating in a democracy as a voting citizen. Yes, the more intelligent youth, in terms of academic ability, can learn these nonsense symbols, but is it education for a modern world?

Just as one example of the ineffectiveness of this approach, we find that youth from 21 to 25 have the poorest voting records in terms of registration and voting of any of the population age groups. It would seem, therefore, that our social studies programs certainly have not encouraged youth to take an active part in their government, and that society, instead of a public education system, must sensitize the young person to finally become a voting member. The greatest privilege of free man, the right to vote at the ballot box, has not been made meaningful to our youth by the discipline-centered approach in our public schools. Yet in spite of all the facts pointing towards the need for massive changes in our high school curricula, the public and the educators who know no other system frantically protect an antiquated and decadent system which ignores the needs of at least 75 percent of the youth enrolled. A man told me recently that his daughter had been taught the metric system three or four times in her school career, each time learned it adequately to the point of passing the test easily, but immediately forgot it since the system was of no use to her in her daily life.

Today's society demands that the high schools serve all youth and that the educational program within that school system be related to today and tomorrow and not to the good old days when only a few students graduated from high school and the rest wandered out into unskilled jobs available in our work force. The industrial revolution brought about a massive increase in goods and services for mankind, but it tended to make man a servant of the machine, feeding the machine, offbearing from the machine. The technological age has made man master of the machine, but there is a price to pay for that mastery; the price is the ability to control and maintain a system of machinery with the labor of serving and offbearing carried out mechanically. The price is the necessity to obtain the education, the job skills, the technical knowledge necessary to enter into employment prior to that employment.

The reorganization of the high school curriculum must provide for a system of vocational exploration to build on the system described previously.

Recent studies indicated conclusively that the problems of providing vocational guidance to students in high school is critical. In a study of the vocational maturity of ninth grade boys, Super and Overstreet[1] found in 1960 that more than half of the students planned to enter occupations that seemed inappropriate for them in terms of intellectual and educational requirements.

Professor Robert Hoppock, of the State University of New York, in a speech before a group of guidance counselors, reported a study of 1685 students in 35 Cincinnati public schools clearly revealed a lack of adequate planning in terms of occupations. The results of this inquiry were reported in these words:

> What would Cincinnati be like if these students became the sole inhabitants of the city in the jobs of their choice ten years from now . . . health services would be very high, with every eighteen people supporting one doctor . . . it may be, however, that they would all be needed in a city which had no garbage disposal workers, no laundry workers, and no water supplies, since no one chose to do that kind of work . . . the two bus drivers . . . will find their customers getting tired of waiting and use the services of the 67 airline pilots. It may be difficult getting to the field to see the 40 baseball players.[2]

Too many educators assume that because youth make such unrealistic choices they are unable to make choices. One guidance authority, Carl McDaniels, took issue in 1968 with the work of other guidance leaders and argued that people in middle teens, ages 14 to 18, *are not too young* to make vocational choices, but

---

[1] D. E. Super and Phoebe L. Overtsreet, *The Vocational Maturity of Ninth Grade Boys* (New York: Columbia University Press, 1960).

[2] Address to the National Seminar on Vocational Guidance, sponsored by the U.S. Office of Education on August 21, 1966, at Northern Michigan University, Marquette.

rather that they are *poorly prepared* to make choices. He refers to the "postponement theory of vocational development" and makes this comment:

> Who needed to make choices? If you stayed in school until graduation you were prepared primarily to go on to further education at the next level . . . today's youth are more highly developed physically and intellectually than any comparable group in recorded history. Today youth learn more and faster than any comparable group in history. It seems that they could also learn to make vocational choices if they were prepared to do so.[3]

Most dropouts occur in high school. At fault is the curriculum; it has little relevance to any of the students and its holding power lies in parental and social pressures to stay in school and the desire of some students to enter college upon graduation. A reorganization of the curriculum at the ninth and tenth grade level, or for youth ages 14 and 15, is necessary if we are to up-date the antiquated high school program. The vocational guidance part of this curriculum must recognize the increased maturity of youth and their readiness to begin to explore tentative occupational choices and their own interests and abilities.

Exploration as a Function of Education

The first "junior high school" was established in Columbus, Ohio. Under the concepts projected for the junior high school, exploration in terms of helping the student find out about self and about possibilities in the world of work was identified as a significant part of the curriculum. In practice, however, the junior high school, instead of achieving the goals and concepts identified for it has become a *junior* high school. The academic disciplines of the high school, modeled after the academic disciplines of the college, have been pushed down into the junior high

---

[3] Carl McDaniels, "Youth: Too Young to Choose," *Vocational Guidance Quarterly*, XVI, No. 4 (June, 1968), 242–49.

school. The junior high school has not really met the goals established for it, and our educational system above the elementary school continues to be a hodge-podge of the subject matter approach prevalent in high school and college, sprinkled with some new subject areas—such as art, music, industrial arts, band—in order to "modernize" the curriculum to present-day needs.

Only one area in the curriculum, industrial arts, has established the concept of exploration as an important goal of the program. The industrial arts program is intended to be a part of the educational program which makes a contribution to the youths' desire to explore the world of work in industry and the jobs available. The industrial arts subject area in the public schools of our state is normally found in grades 7 through 12, but it has had such a hodge-podge of goals, curriculum emphasis, and variety of facilities and equipment in the various schools that it seems to have little influence as a significant exploration function in most of the public schools in our system.

The birdbox-hatrack-bookcase orientation of the industrial arts program might have been an orientation to the wood-centered economy of the early 1900's, but it certainly doesn't have relationship to an exploratory program for our modern technological society. Even though the industrial arts program has not normally served the function for which it was planned, there are some schools in which the exploration function of industrial arts has been a significant factor in providing students with experiences of a tryout nature to enable them to evaluate their interests and abilities in that area.

Some school districts have maintained a broad exploratory industrial arts program. The industrial arts program at the seventh and eighth grade level can be involved as a part of the career orientation program described in the preceding chapter, and an industrial arts program built around exploration of certain facets of the world of work could be an integral part of a system of vocational guidance at grades nine and ten for youth who are interested in exploring such areas for the purpose of career choice. For some unfathomable reason, the public education system has accepted the concept of industrial arts as an exploratory function and as a part of the school curriculum, but has ignored the need for exploration in relationships to the other broad areas of work. The issue I want to present here is that, in principle, the educational system accepts the function of exploration in the industrial arts area, but generally relegates it to the basement level area of the curriculum in which it is an adjunct, or treats it as a supplement to the curriculum rather than a part of the core.

If the concept is accepted in the industrial arts area, what about the opportunities to explore areas of business, marketing, health, agriculture, personal service relating to all levels of employment, including the professions? I believe sincerely that exploration is a function of the educational program and that exploration at the level of the ninth and tenth year, or ages 14 and 15, should be a function of personal choice, not assignments. If we accept the concept of exploration as a function of the educational program, then why should it not be available on a personal choice basis over the wide spectrum of the occupational community? I concur with educators who believe that the reason youth have made immature choices is that youth have not been given a systematic method of developing the proper attitudes toward work, an understanding of the world of work, or an opportunity to explore certain functions in that world of work in relation to their interests and abilities.

Throughout this book I have stressed the concept of experience as an essential base for all learning. It certainly holds true that experience is an essential part of the area of exploration. I reject entirely the concept presently prevalent in guidance circles that the presentation of occupational information to youth is an effective method of assisting youth to make choices. The preoccupation of the guidance service area with the informational approach seems to have been founded on several assumptions:

1) That informational data on jobs listed in written form is authentic and communicates facts about work.
2) That specific information about occupations in terms of working conditions, pay, status, etc., are valid for today and applicable for tomorrow.
3) That the reading of data or information about jobs meets significant student needs and produces significant behavior patterns.

4) That occupational information serves as a basis for action decisions on a "reason" basis.

I believe that these assumptions are without basis in research and do not hold up under any rule of reason. Educational theory based upon principles of learning growing out of psychological studies point to experience and personal involvement as the basis for learning. Yet these false assumptions furnish the basis for much of the existing vocational guidance practices in our public schools. Discussions with guidance people would lead me to believe that more money has been invested in the area of occupational information than in any other area of the field of guidance and counseling. What is the basis in learning theory to support such an emphasis? I would suggest the development of a broad vocational exploration program as the core or center of the curriculum for the ninth and tenth years of our educational system. Such a program should involve a significant portion of the student's time and could be the core or base around which certain of the other educational areas, such as mathematics and science, could function.

A Broad Practical Arts Program

In the terminology of educators, the vocational exploration curriculum described above might be defined as a "practical arts" program. The term practical arts has been used in reference to the exploratory function and most generally the only practical arts program available in the school has been the very limited and often confused program of industrial arts.

It is my judgement that without a broad vocational exploratory or a broad practical arts program, the public school is denying the student an important experience in his educational career at the point at which the student assumes responsibility for and control of his educational and vocational future.

I reject the necessity for preparing the young person at the ninth grade level for employment as an auto mechanic through a vocational education program, just as I reject the importance of initiating a college preparatory program at this level. This state-

ment is made on the basis that most of the young persons in the
ninth grade are about 14 years of age. Guidance studies would
indicate that most youth at age 14 lack the maturity for making a
career judgement and their physical development often does not
enable them to participate effectively in a vocational program.

I am not speaking of the 16 year old in the ninth grade. Boys
or girls at age 16 should be afforded the opportunity of participating in a vocational training program regardless of the grade level in
which they are enrolled. I believe that most guidance counselors
will agree with me the 14 year old is too young to make an occupational choice and to enroll in a vocational program. But they
seem to ignore the fact that a college preparatory program is
equally as narrow and limited in its approach to subject matter. In
addition, the college preparatory program does not provide an
experience base for the instruction provided in the various disciplines.

The nature of our technological world denies the youth experience at home or in employment as a basis for the choice of a
vocation. The public school therefore must accept the responsibility
for assisting the youth in evaluating self and selecting occupational
goals. We must extend the walls of the school to include the entire
community. A limited number of jobs available to youth in the
business sector of our economy and the paid work experience made
available by cooperative programs between school and industry,
must not limit experience provided the student in the world of
work. The concept of experience should be extended to include
observation and voluntary experiences in those kinds of community
situations in which work for pay is forbidden by laws, union regulations, or practical considerations. The extension of the walls of the
schools to include the community will benefit not only the students,
but also the teachers. Through such a program, teachers will gain
a better understanding of the world of work which will provide
employment to the youth upon the completion of their educational
program.

Any successful exploratory program must be based on the
concept that all work is honorable. Dr. Paul Briggs, Superintendent
of Schools in Cleveland, in a meeting in my office with the superintendents of the eight major cities, reported on a dentist who gave

up a successful practice to become chief custodian of one of the schools on the basis that he got tired of looking into people's mouths. It is possible that if this person had had an opportunity to get acquainted with the nature of the occupation or profession to which he was aspiring he might have found that his interests were not in this direction, even though he was intellectually capable of completing the curriculum necessary to become a dentist.

Another member of my staff told me about a child of one of his relatives who had established for himself the goal of becoming a neurosurgeon. This young person, a very able student, asked the question however, "How do I know that I want to be a neurosurgeon?" Nothing in the educational curriculum of the wealthy suburban school provided him with any opportunity to determine if he had the personal interests and capabilities which would enable him to become a competent neurosurgeon—nothing in the school program, despite the fact that essentially twelve years of education beyond high school would be necessary before the person could accomplish the goal of becoming a neurosurgeon. This young person worked to form an Explorer's Scout group which would have an experience in the hospital as a part of its program, so that he could learn something about the working of the health area in general and the medical profession in particular. The boy proved that he was more resourceful than the curriculum. From the ingenious ideas of some of our youth we could learn how to develop the type of practical arts program as an integral part of a system of vocational guidance and vocational education.

The industrial arts personnel in our public schools are capable of organizing and participating in a phase of the practical arts programs related to industry. The goals and objectives of the industrial arts program, however, are so loosely interpreted, the facilities are so haphazardly provided, and the curriculum time investment so small at the ninth and tenth grade level for those who choose to enroll, that the present program often cannot be an effective part of the vocational exploration program envisioned here. The industrial arts program, however, in cooperation with the vocational guidance people, might logically be the first section of the school curriculum which can be converted to provide for a very significant input to a total practical arts program. The practical arts program, however, cannot be justified if it is limited to the industrial area, since the industrial area represents only a part, even if it is a significant part, of the vocational opportunities in our modern world.

I believe it is important to recognize the other broad occupational categories important to our economy in order that the school can program significant experiences in school and out of school as a part of the broad practical arts program. The field of business education has for years provided youth at the ninth- and tenth-grade level with practical experience in typing skills. Such instruction has been limited essentially to skills for personal use and as a lead-in to the secretarial type of program offered on a cafeteria basis in the eleventh and twelfth years. Many girls interested in the area of business have used this loosely knit program as essentially a tryout function for the field of business. The preoccupation with skills at the ninth and tenth grade level, however, and the total relationship of these to the essentially secretarial and clerical occupations, has provided the students with limited opportunities to learn about the other broad areas of employment related to the business field. Studies by the business educators indicate that in order to achieve at the secretarial level, the girl would need to be above average in intelligence. Does this, then, limit the field of business and office education to the select group who are above average in intelligence? The experiences in vocational education programming in the field of business opens up the employment opportunities to a broad range of interest and ability levels. The vocational business and office education people in our state recognize the following occupational areas or occupational codes as defining programs so that curricula can be organized around each area to prepare youth to enter a number of different jobs in the economy.

Instructional Codes Most Frequently Used
in Business and Office Education Programs
at the High School Level

14.0100   Accounting and Computing
14.0200   Business Data Processing Systems
14.0301   Duplicating Operator
14.0302   Clerical Services

14.0303 General Office Clerk
14.0399 Office Machines Operator
14.0700 Clerk Stenographer
14.0900 Clerk Typist
14.9999 OWE Program Type 30
14.1000 COE Unplaced Students

It would seem feasible that, to have meaning to youth looking to business, a practical arts program should provide the person with an opportunity to explore all of these broad areas of business and office education in order to match their interests and abilities with the job opportunities. As an example, while it would normally take a student of above-average ability to succeed in the secretarial occupations, a girl with a dull-normal achievement level on intelligence measurements might achieve, if properly motivated, in the area of office duplicating. An interesting point is that the girl in office duplicating may make more money upon graduation than the girl in the secretarial area.

Another broad area for inclusion in the practical arts program would be in the area of marketing goods and services produced in our economy. This area would normally be concerned with the flow of goods and services to the market and the sales of such goods to the people on a wholesale or retail basis. Approximately 15 percent of our people are employed in the area of distribution, which represents a significant part of our employed area. Perhaps the highest paying jobs in our economy are in the area of sales, yet what part of our school program encourages youth to review the area of sales of goods and services as a future occupation? Too many of our educators believe that anybody can be a salesman, that training isn't important, that people only go into this occupation if they can't do something else. It may be true if you are talking about the ribbon clerk in the corner specialty store, but our industries and businesses could not stay open if no one sold the goods and services that they produce. This broad field of distribution and marketing, therefore, needs to be included in the practical arts program as an area for exploration. Community resources and simulated types of activities would be essential to provide the kind of experiences to enable the young person to check his interest and capabilities in the field of distribution.

The field of agriculture covers much more than the area of production agriculture in our modern economy. Occupations in the area of horticulture, floriculture, landscape gardening, nursery work, agriculture businesses and services, agriculture mechanics, all offer opportunities for employment in addition to the very important area of agriculture production. Too many people would view this area of exploration as related only to rural America. The largest vocational agricultural program in the public schools of Ohio, planned to prepare youth for employment in agricultural jobs, exists in the city of Cleveland, Ohio, one of the nation's fifteen major cities.

Many of the hangups we have in terms of occupations have been based upon the limited understanding and experiences of the people educating our youth. While the number of people producing foods and fiber in our nation has decreased, the numbers of people to serve those producers, handle the products, and preserve the environmental quality of an affluent society have maintained the importance of agricultural occupations in our economy. The occupations represented, then, in the essential agriculture areas relating to the producing of foods and fiber, and the related occupational areas for sales, service, and beautification deserve the attention of our public schools and deserve to be included as a facet of the practical arts program for a modern age.

The areas of personal and health services are of growing importance in our affluent society, as we now have more people working in services than in production. Our economy must have sanitary workers, food handlers, laundry workers, doctors, dentists, nurses, aides and a host of other personal service occupations. The areas of personal and health services, therefore, must be a significant part of the practical arts program and again will need to involve experiences in the community as well as in the school.

The industrial area covered by the industrial arts program would perhaps include three areas of emphasis: construction, manufacturing and repair. Such occupational areas as carpentry, plumbing, bricklaying and sheet metal would be represented in the construction trade area. Machine shop, welding, and foundry would be included in the manufacturing section. Related occupations such as auto mechanics, electronics, machine maintenance, hydraulic repair and a host of other service occupations would be included in the broad category of repair services.

The program of vocational exploration envisioned here cannot be achieved in the two periods per week assigned to a facility with limited program concepts, limited facilities, and little teacher time available. The concept of the vocational education exploration program is not one of addition to the present curriculum, but an insert into the very core of the curriculum which would require a major change in the total educational program at grades nine and ten.

No less than an hour and a half a day of the school program should be alloted to this practical arts program in order that the student, over a two-year period, could have the opportunity to explore in depth those areas which he or she chooses to explore. The time emphasis suggested here also recognizes that a portion of the exploratory curriculum may take place in the community through observations or through participation, when such participation is in accordance with the child-labor laws or the rules and regulations of the community institutions involved.

I do not suggest here the employment of a new faculty in addition to the present faculty, but the reorientation of existing faculty and curriculum. Perhaps the industrial arts teachers and the existing business and office education teachers are the most obvious group that can be involved quickly and directly into the practical arts program, but the mere assignment of teachers to a responsibility will be of no value unless the curriculum, the facilities, school-community relationships and equipment are made available to implement the concepts. The vocational teachers, the home economics teachers, the science teachers, the social studies teachers, all represent resources of personnel to adapt and adjust to staffing of the practical arts program. Guidance counselors could serve an important function as planning, coordinating and supportive staff.

I would emphasize here that we are *not* talking about only a practical emphasis to a subject-centered curriculum, but an experience-centered emphasis to a practical arts program. The students' choices, the students' goals, should be the basis for a flexible curriculum in which personal experiences of a laboratory- or community-based program would be the starting point for any written occupational information or studies that would be made available.

Yes, new materials would need to be developed. Yes, additional equipment would need to be provided. Yes, remodeling of the school facilities would be necessary. Yes, liaison between the school and community would become vital. But the alternative of continuing an educational system which is not relevant to todays needs and which is rushing toward a welfare society is much more costly.

I have been discussing the matter of a broad practical arts program which is essentially a vocational exploration program at the heart of the curriculum, but I have purposely left the function of the guidance counselor in this program until the end of the program suggestions. This is done deliberately on the basis that the guidance counselor, as important as he may be, is only a part of the program, but through his efforts may serve a planning and coordinating function, pulling all parts of the effort together. The specific curricular input of the vocational guidance counselor would be to have a continuing relationship with the students to guide their participation in the entire practical arts program and direct involvement with the students at some time in the program in order to help the students look critically at their abilities and interests in relationship to occupational goals. A student's realistic evaluation of self on a positive basis certainly is an essential component of occupational choice.

I agree, as do guidance people, with the concept of free choice by the individual, but I don't believe that there is even a semblance of free choice unless the person has enough personal experiences in relation to work, enough information about opportunities, and enough information about self, to make a free choice. Any choice made upon inadequate information or experiences is not free; it is guided, and may have status considerations or parental or community pressures as its only basis. I can envision a program of practical arts in which the laboratories are established on the broad basis, with competent personnel staffing those laboratories, with students flowing from experience to experience, with provisions for experiences in the community, with the guidance counselor having a contact with the student at the close of each vocational exploration experience. They could be the true professional leaders of the curriculum-centered programming for vocational exploration.

Supplemental Assistance Needed

I have suggested in the other phases of the work-centered program that this program of vocational exploration will not be broadly implemented unless there is leadership at the state level which can bring together the types of people that can put the meaningful experiences into the program described above. Again I would stress that the leadership must come from the State Department of Education, rather than from other professional sources, such as the university, in order to make an impact upon school systems in all parts of the state and to package the program in such a manner that necessary funding for the program can be presented in an organized fashion to the legislature. It is very possible that the division of vocational education, through the availability of state and federal funds assigned to such divisions, could initiate the necessary pilot programs in order to arrive at a pattern or patterns that would be effective for services to youth in all schools.

I believe that there must be some additional investments in pilot programs based again on the concept of supplementing existing educational expenditures in order to implement the new concepts, rather than purchasing an entirely new educational program. Action takes place when an able person with staff resources available to him is assigned the responsibility for program development and implementation. It would be feasible, therefore, to suggest that the Division of Guidance and Testing and the Division of Vocational Education in the State Department of Education be assigned the responsibility of cooperatively developing a broad program of vocational exploration. There is no question that there would need to be an investment in curriculum organization and in curriculum material development. Pilot programming would be desirable, however, before broad dollars are invested in curriculum and curriculum materials.

While it is possible that several patterns might evolve regarding the practical arts program, instructional materials developed on a statewide or nationwide basis in relationship to the broad areas discussed above could probably be used in several different patterns of program organization. Development of such materials are costly and materials for new programs do not normally attract investments from publishers. If this program is implemented in such a manner that every student will have an opportunity to participate, the commercial publishers will find it feasible to develop very adequate and meaningful materials for use in the public schools. Perhaps a representative from the publishers' group should be involved in the planning committees at the state level, looking towards the implementation of the programs.

Since the program proposed is significantly different from any educational program now being offered in our schools, there would need to be an involvement of teachers in in-service education programs to prepare them for participation in the vocational exploration program. Such in-service education should perhaps be on the basis of the schools in which the program is to be initiated, rather than an in-service program provided at a central source such as a university. The in-service educational program, offered on an individual school basis, would enable the teachers to develop into a working team rather than to function as independent units in the educational program. Any movement to make such major changes in the curriculum as suggested here would be successful only if the teachers are involved.

Again, the key to the success of the program will be the principal of the individual school who is responsible for the scheduling of the courses at that school and the leadership of the staff group. Without the support of the principal, all desires on the part of superintendents of instruction at the local level, the state department of education or the state legislature will go for naught. The principal represents the educational leadership in the individual school and can make or break a program. This does not negate the importance of the central staff in the local school district, including resource services of the guidance and vocational units in that system. Regional and statewide meetings of principals can be instrumental in encouraging this educational change within the local communities.

State and local committees, involving parents, professions and public are essential in the development of this program. The local committees should involve heavy representation from industries and businesses in the communities, including the public service agencies, since their facilities are now important to the individual student in programs of exploration.

The schools will need additional funds in order to implement the curriculum and to provide for additional cost necessitated by the broad expansion of an experience-centered vocational exploration program. Such additional cost could be covered by special grants tied to the number of students enrolled in the school, since it would be expected that all students would be provided with this exploration experience and expected to participate in the experience. Another procedure would be to provide a bonus amount as part of the per-pupil allocation or classroom unit allocation if the state has a foundation program. Any state assistance, however, should be tied to plans submitted to the state department of education by the schools, indicating how they intend to make the vocational exploration program available to all students.

Minimum standards for such a program should provide that all students will be involved and given an average of an hour and a half daily over the period of the ninth and tenth years to participate in this vocational exploration program. Committees at the state level should develop the types of minimum standards which would insure the students an adequate program in each school district in keeping with their needs, not in keeping with the existing organizational pattern that is now hopelessly out of date.

A Proposal

The Division of Vocational Education in our state has developed guidelines for the establishment of career exploration programs in grades 9 and 10, or for youth 14 and 15 years old. Priority is to be given to those school systems that have developed career orientation programs described in the preceding chapter and who submit proposals for World of Work programs for K-6 grades in the elementary schools as described in Chapter V.

The guidelines, as for previous innovative programs in the proposed system of vocational guidance and vocational education, were developed with the assistance of a statewide committee involving junior high and high school principals, vocational educators, guidance counselors, counselor educators, secondary school educators, and others.

The guidelines forwarded to schools for the career exploration program are as follows:

I. *Statement of Purpose*

This particular guideline establishes the format and approval procedures of proposals from school districts by the Vocational Division to cover the programs that are proposed for students in grades 9-10, or all 14-15 year olds not in an Occupational Work Adjustment program.*

It is the purpose of this program to provide in-depth exploration for all 9-10th grades or 14-15 year old youth in career clusters of their choosing following a successful career orientation at the 7-8th grade levels. These students will have exploratory experiences in the school in selected fields of the "World of Work" and include those necessary experiences outside the school that will provide the first-hand observation or experience relevant to today's society. The philosophy of the program entails the involvement of all students in grades 9-10 in the schools selected. Breadth of program will of necessity require the use of facilities and activities beyond the school walls both in finding personnel and in providing experiences for the students. This may include cooperation with other schools and school personnel within and without the school district.

II. *Proposal Submission*

1. A written plan may be submitted by any school district in Ohio that is currently operating a Vocational Education program.

---

* Author's note: The Occupational Work Adjustment Program is described in a subsequent chapter.

2. The plan proposal will be reviewed by a panel of consultants called to the Division of Vocational Education, State Department of Education.
3. Plan proposals will be recommended for approval by the panel, and finally approved for operation and reimbursement by the Division.
4. Plans shall be mailed no later than June 1.
5. Design and implementation of the plan must provide for the enrollment and participation of all 9-10th grade students in any one school(s).
6. Plans should include an opportunity for students to learn more about their *measured* aptitudes and interests.
7. Format of proposal shall be as follows:
   A. Description of program.
   B. Organization and administration of program shall be described.
   C. Timetables and schedules of operation including student schedules shall be included.
   D. A list of advisory committee members should be submitted with proposal which also includes employers in the community.
   E. Facilities that will be used shall be listed, by building, including room description and other factors when related to employers.
   F. Budget requested shall be by breakdown of expenditures required over and above regular school costs. Budget request and listing should be in accordance with reimbursement standards listed in Part V.

III. *Minimum Requirements for Proposals*

1. Programs requested shall cover the two years (9-10th grades), and shall be designed for all students in these grades, including any other 14-15 year olds where possible regardless of grade level.
2. Programs shall include a minimum of 270 clock hours of instruction in the two-year period in an acceptable pattern of scheduling. Time may be scheduled in standard periods per day in a block of time (but *not* in a 1-period per day for the 2 years). Any blocking principle may be used to equate to minimum hours (i.e., a 4th quarter useage, or x-number of days/weeks on a full-time basis, etc.). On-the-job work experience may be used in the requested

hours as long as it is supervised by the school, and hopefully will be in excess of the minimum hours required for the two years.

3. Programs shall include "hands-on" exploration in laboratories, on-the-job, and/or classes in any combination or configuration.

4. Each student shall have the chance to explore at least 3 clusters of occupations in the two years.

5. In-school laboratories may consist of individual rooms, industrial arts areas, home economic labs, business education rooms, or other designated areas and facilities. Laboratories may be un-used vocational facilities or stations provided by industry, business, or professional groups.

6. Programs should progress from the 7-8th grade Career Orientation Program (or similar) through exploration of clusters, and must include hands-on experiences as a basis for exploration.

7. Programs shall be of such size to warrant breadth of job clusters in the occupational codes of the USOE as typified in the publication VOCATIONAL EDUCATION AND OCCUPATIONS or in the USDL publication DICTIONARY OF OCCUPATIONAL TITLES (DOT). It may be that this breadth will require a multi-school approach or an "area" school approach.

IV. *Evaluation of Program*

1. Evaluation shall be made of program at the middle (progress report) and end of each year.

2. The evaluation shall indicate areas of career exploration completed, statistics on program, and other items such as analysis by consulting teachers and outside visitations. It should show failures and problems as well as successes.

3. There shall be a student evaluation of the program.

4. There shall be a parent evaluation of the program.

5. If community observations or work experiences are used, there shall be an employer evaluation.

6. Plans for evaluation should include provisions for determining changes in students' occupational interests, attitudes, and knowledge from the beginning to the end of the program.

V. *Reimbursement Standards*

1. Programs shall be reimbursed at the end of the year based on a regular affidavit submitted to the Division of Vocational Education, State Department of Education.

2. Additional costs of the program will probably be in the areas of coordination, materials, transportation, retirement costs, and teaching aids. Other costs can be submitted for approval if justified, but all costs will have to be supplemental and may not supplant present costs.

3. In-Service training of personnel may be included in these pilot projects. Costs shall be identified in budgets and itemized on reimbursement.

4. Maximum budget may be established at no more than $30 per student, or on a class basis for each year of operation. Only pilot projects will be funded at this time after their approval.

VI. *Personnel*

1. Coordinators of programs shall be qualified as approved Vocational Education teachers or Vocational Guidance Counselors, or as otherwise identified and documented as to qualifications.

2. An in-service program should be conducted for all teachers participating in the project and teaching in the program in order to assure some degree of success in the program.

3. External personnel and consultants utilized in off-school situations must be screened to meet the needs of the program, including the on-the-job supervisor when co-op work experience is used.

Note: Occupational Work Adjustment teachers and students may be exempt from this program if in existence in the school where the program will operate.

These are pilot projects for experimental and demonstration purposes ONLY.

SUMMARY

The concept of work as a motivating factor in the life of the youth, as well as the adult life, has been well-documented. The problems of inadequate and unreasonable occupational choice on the part of the youth as they approach the age of 16 may not be so much a problem of the immaturity of the youth as it is rigidity in the educational system. We can point to the immature occupational goals of the youth, but fail to point to the fact that the schools almost completely ignore the needs of youth to develop vocational choices through an experience-centered curriculum. The history of our high school educational program has tied in so completely with college entrance requirements, in themselves no longer valid, that it tends to ignore the needs of 75 percent of the youth enrolled.

Perhaps in years gone by, the high school program was not even important in our society. Today, the high school is important for all youth and massive efforts must be made to make the curriculum relevant. In this chapter I have proposed the development of another step in the system of vocational guidance and vocational education for youth at the ninth and tenth grade, or 14 and 15 year, level. I suggest that this vocational exploration curriculum at this level again be curriculum-centered and teacher-centered, rather than guidance-counselor-centered.

The exploration program should cover the broad areas of construction, manufacturing, repair services, business, distribution, marketing, agriculture and personal services. It is suggested that this vocational exploration program be at the core of the educational curriculum for grades 9 and 10 and that an average of one and one-half hours per day over the period of the two years be made available to the students for the purpose of exploration. The exploration should be under the control of the student, not of the teacher or guidance counselor. I suggest that the existing staff serve as the basis for the staffing for the exploration program. The staff should be prepared for the new responsibilities through in-service training and the provision for supplemental materials and leadership, rather than the employment of a totally new and additional staff. The vocational guidance counselor, while not *the* system of vocational exploration, plays a greater planning and coordinating role in this phase of the vocational guidance system than in previous phases.

Under the system of vocational exploration proposed it is important that the student analyze his own self-interests and abilities as he participates in the exploration of various families of occupations. It is in this role of self-evaluation and in the role of coordinating each student's participation in the vocational exploration program that the vocational guidance counselor has a significant contact with each of the students enrolled.

In this phase of the system of vocational guidance and vocational education we are again talking about a program for all youth and involving not only the school facilities, but also the community. The goal of this phase of the program is to assist many and perhaps most of the youth to make tentative vocational choices in order that the last two years in the high school curriculum can be best directed towards achieving these goals.

Chapter 8

A WORK ADJUSTMENT PROGRAM FOR UNDER-ACHIEVERS, GRADES NINE AND TEN, AGES 14 AND 15

The Dropout-Prone Youth

Education is the only profession that can fail to serve the clients, blame the clients and their parents for their failures, then throw the failure out on society. The educational system has been so busy maintaining its standards, based upon the successes of youth who would probably be successful in spite of the educational system, that it has not bothered with that group of students who have not been able to jump the artificial educational hurdles based on questionable concepts.

Teachers too often pass on to the next grade the students who have not achieved the basic skills of reading, writing and arithmetic necessary for success in that grade. The teachers at the next level in turn pass on the inadequately prepared student to the next grade, and so on until the young person is old enough to drop out of school. Who can blame the teachers? They are overloaded by student numbers and have little available in the way of remedial services for either physical or educational needs of the students.

These pass-me-ons know that they are being cheated in the educational system. All students from low-socio-economic families can do is suffer the degrading indignities of this process and look forward to the day when they can leave the system. The more affluent resort to tutoring, private schools or pressuring of the educational system to do something to aid their youngster. In both cases, however, the students and the parents are led to believe that they are inadequate, that they should be ashamed of themselves, and how dare anyone question the omnipotence of the educational system? No one wants to wear a dunce cap, whether that dunce cap is placed there by the teacher or by the attitudes of the other students because of lack of ability to achieve in the system. The seedbed for the early dropouts from our public schools is in the early years of the educational system.

We not only have dropouts. We have *pushouts, throwouts,* and *shoveouts* who have long ago been abandoned by the system and who will leave that system when they can no longer stand the indignities imposed upon them by the system, or put up with the antiquated educational offerings made available to them by that system. Many of the dropouts from our schools do not lack the capacities to complete school—they just lack the will to continue to run a meaningless race.

Children from all economic levels look forward to participating in the educational program. For those in the lower socio-economic group, education represents their only way out of the pit of poverty. Yet some of the young people who dropped out of that system, years later, disillusioned and somewhat dishonored, marked for life, told us at Mahoning Valley, "They done us out. They knew we couldn't read or write or figure, but they passed us on." Our experiences at Mahoning Valley Vocational School proved to us that over half of the young people enrolled in that residential center for school dropouts had something wrong with them that would prevent them from participating ably in the educational program. Over 50 percent of the people at Mahoning Valley were eligible for vocational rehabilitation. Can you imagine how it would feel as you entered the door of the school in the morning to know that that school branded you a failure, and that for the full day in that school center you would be looked upon by students and teachers as a failure? How long would you be able to hold up your head in such a situation? Would you be able to continue to be a good citizen in that school? What kind of shell would you have to build around you to ward off the stinging reminders of your inadequacies?

The dropout-prone youth, age 9 or 10, is behind his grade level in reading and educational achievement. He is resentful of the system. As he finds that the last chance for relevance to his needs really offers nothing for his benefit except more meaningless subjects, he is ready to vote against the system with his feet. The system has failed to serve this youth, to serve his educational, social or psychological needs. The educational system has left him with a self-concept of failure. It has socially branded the family of the child. In the middle class this blow is one which greatly strains total family relationships, as they interpret it as a blow to their status in the community. In the lower socio-economic groups, the branding of their child as a failure is just another evidence that the system has no real concern for them as people.

Twenty-four out of every one hundred young people starting the first grade fail to graduate from high school in Ohio. I would judge that this rate, nationwide, is much the same. Within the inner-city sections of our major cities, however, this dropout rate may approximate 50 percent of the young people starting the first grade, with the dropouts adding power to the social dynamite already existing in those areas. Non-whites represent the major percentage of the population in our ghettos and a significant portion of the poverty group outside of our major cities. The issue takes on added significance when we realize that the percentage of increase of 16- to 24-year olds in the labor force during the period 1965–70 was greater for the non-white than for the white.

We have learned from our experiences at the residential center at Mahoning Valley Vocational School that young people who dropped out of school realize the importance of education and will participate in reading, writing and arithmetic if that type of education is related to their goals and their needs. We also learned that young people who had been discipline problems in their education program ceased to be discipline problems when they were kept busy for 100 percent of the time in relevant educational programs —that is, relevant to their concerns for earning a living.

I am suggesting that our educational system must establish the pattern of zero dropouts from that system. It has the same obligation as any other profession to find a means of serving the client in a manner which will bring benefit to the client.

Occupational Choice Related to Age

Experiences with vocational programs indicate the dropout rates in vocational programs are significantly lower than the dropout rates for the normal population. A recent study in Cleveland, Ohio proved this to be true in the inner-city sections of the major cities. A study by the Cleveland school district, covering an inner-city school, showed a dropout rate of 8 percent of the general school population in the period of time covered by the study, while the dropout rate from the vocational programs in the same school was 1.7 to 1.8 percent.

Experiences indicate that enrollment in the vocational program shows meaning and relevance for the students enrolled. Yet research in guidance shows that youth at the age of 14 do not have the maturity to make a proper vocational choice in the light of their abilities, interests and job opportunities available. The program suggested in the preceding chapter is proposed for 14 and 15 year olds, grades 9 and 10, to lead them to an occupational choice for enrollment in a goal-centered program at age 16. Superintendents of our major cities, however, pointed up that many of the young people who badly needed vocational education would not be around at age 16 to participate in the program since they became disillusioned at age 14 and 15 and dropped out of school before they were eligible to enter a vocational program. School systems faced with a massive number of youth, particularly in the inner city, who were dropout-prone at age 14 and 15, asked that some type of vocational programming be provided for these young people in order to maintain them within the school program.

Placement of the dropout-prone youth into the regular program which is geared to the normal youth who is willing to adjust to the system does little except to increase his antagonism towards society and to decrease his self-concept. Experiences indicate that with the proper motivation, even the educationally mentally retarded can achieve in many occupations that we formerly considered far beyond their abilities. The motivation for further achievement does not occur as a part of a failure sequence, but as a part of a success sequence. Success is the key to motivation of youth, and motivation is the key to social and educational adjustment. We must, therefore, provide experiences for youth which enable them to see themselves as worthy members of our society able to contribute and participate in that society as equals.

A person's self-concept plays an important role in his achievements and his adjustment to that society. I wonder what the failure syndrome of our public schools is doing to the self-concepts of millions of our youth. We place them into a position in which, if they question the system, the system points toward a small group of young people in the school who have been able to achieve in the abstract knowledge demanded by the school, and through this method makes them feel inferior. We deprive them of their manhood and womanhood as equal citizens in the society and forever brand them as rejects.

The Work Adjustment Program as a Tool

The Occupational Work Adjustment program that I propose here is not a vocational education program. It is a program of work adjustment which uses work as a means of enabling a person to find that he can achieve something, that he can be a significant participating member of society. The program that I am proposing here, therefore, is more a part of the system of vocational guidance. The program would permit students to gain the type of self-respect and adjustment to the educational program that would enable them to make some of the same choices as the students completing the work exploration program described in the preceding chapter.

We must accept the concept that all people are worthy recipients of the benefit of the total educational system and that if we concur with the studies in guidance, age 16 is about the earliest time for a reasonable occupational choice. We must maintain students in school until age 16 and provide relevant education for all, relevant to their needs and goals.

In addition to the problems of the curriculum in relationship to school-disoriented youth, there is also a problem that the normal public school schedule divides the student among a number of different teachers during the day. How can young people talk to their teachers in school if all they can talk about is their failure to achieve at the level demanded by that teacher? I am afraid that I, too, would be belligerent towards a school and society which continually identified me as a failure.

As we worked with the dropouts enrolled in the residential center at Mahoning Valley, they told us, "No one cared about us." None of the students to whom we talked had ever been served by a guidance counselor. What an indictment of our public school system when the very people who probably need service most from a guidance counselor receive no service from such a counselor!

A new type of program has been introduced into public schools of Ohio this year which I believe will make a significant contribution to our system of vocational guidance and vocational education. It is planned specifically for the dropout-prone youth at ages 14 and 15, or those enrolled in grades 9 and 10. It is based on the concept of work adjustment through work in school or in the community and the relationship of the dropout-prone youth for a half day with a person who "cares." The occupational work adjustment program is designed to serve youth who may not be in school long enough to enroll in vocational education unless their attitudes towards that school program can be adjusted. The program is aimed specifically at helping such dropout-prone youth become reoriented and motivated toward education and to explore careers directly through work experience. This program is funded as an additional vocational unit under our Division of Vocational Education, and this first year thirty different schools have participated in the program. Within a period of six months this program has gained recognition for the outstanding services provided to such people, to the point where we will be initiating additional programs in the middle of the year, contrary to our normal pattern of operation.

The forward-looking concepts of the laws governing the work of women and minors in Ohio enables youth at this age level to do certain kinds of non-hazardous work in the community. Through the efforts of our Division of Vocational Education in the State Department and the help of William Parry, an industrialist in Akron, Ohio, who has a great concern for work-oriented youth, the Department of Labor has approved an experimental program in five states which will enable the youth enrolled in such work adjustment programs to not only work within the school system, but also to work at non-hazardous occupations in the community. We believe that a significant part of the success of this program is the involvement of the youth in work that they see is meaningful and needed by society, and which returns to them some remuneration.

In one program in Dayton, Ohio a 14-year-old boy, shy, but old beyond his years, told a visiting inspecting team that as a result of his "job" in the Work Adjustment program, he had saved thirty dollars, and that for the first time that he could remember his six brothers and sisters would all have a gift on Christmas.

Every work-adjustment program of the type discussed here must have at the heart of that program work experience in a job. Some examples of job stations in which students are placed are: cafeterias, bus garages for service, librarians, custodians, office helpers, teacher aides—any honest work in which the student can have a successful experience and which makes some small contribution to the on-going activities of society.

Organization and Operation

As stated above, this program is in operation and can serve as a center of the curriculum around which the rest of the educational program can adjust. Instruction in this program is under the direction of an occupational work adjustment teacher-coordinator, who instructs the students in the classroom on concepts related to job adjustment, as well as supervises and counsels them in their work experience placement in the school or in the community. In-class instruction is aimed at helping the student to become work oriented and to continue his education toward a career goal. Instruction is offered in job adjustment and job performance information, as well as remedial instruction in academic subjects. The students enrolled in a program spend at least two forty-five minute periods per day in this classroom instruction under the coordinator and have a minimum of two hours, or two periods, each day for on-the-job experience at various work stations throughout the school system or in the community. In addition, students receive instruction in other required subjects geared to their comprehension level and interests in the half of the school day not covered by the program. A strong suggestion is made to the schools that the subjects in the half day outside the work adjustment program should be correlated with the work of the student in the occupational work adjustment program.

The work adjustment teacher-coordinator identifies the work stations, assists students with their first contacts with the employers in the work stations, and through visitation to the student at work, coordinates and gives general supervision to the student on the job. The student, however, works under the direct supervision of the work sponsors in school or in the community. The observations by the teacher-coordinator of the student on the job serves as a basis for counseling in the school period to help the youth to develop good work habits and work performance. The work employer and work adjustment teacher-coordinator both are concerned with the evaluation of the student progress. It is required that schools considering this program should have in operation a well-planned program of guidance and testing services as a means of helping to identify students who can benefit from the program. It is also required that the vocational programs be made available to the students upon completion of this occupational work adjustment program which will enable them to progress into a vocational training program.

Physical facilities needed for this program are minimal. The schools are expected to furnish adequate classroom facilities for the occupational work adjustment program. Classrooms need to contain tables, chairs, chalkboards, bulletin boards, storage cabinets, filing cabinets, as well as a desk and telephone for the work adjustment teacher-coordinator. A glass-enclosed conference area within or immediately adjacent to classroom is desirable. Such an area is needed by the work adjustment teacher-coordinator for individual student counseling while the class is in session. Adequate supplies, such as programmed learning and remedial reading materials should be available for the use of the instructor. The time schedule for the work adjustment program is as follows:

A. Two forty-five minute periods arranged concurrently, devoted to classroom work adjustment and related instruction.
B. A minimum of two periods, or two hours per day, devoted to work stations within the school or within the community.
C. The balance of the day devoted to regularly required general subjects or other subjects designed to meet the individual needs of these students and to be geared to his or her level of comprehension, interests and needs.

All work adjustment teacher-coordinators are required to participate in an in-service teacher education program which includes a seminar prior to the service as a teacher-coordinator. It is difficult to determine the qualifications necessary for a successful work adjustment teacher-coordinator. We are sure that the major qualifications for success are those that cannot be identified by written qualifications based upon education and experience, as the true test is the adjustment of the individual to the youth and the empathy that he can develop in relationship to him. However, minimum qualifications have been established for the selection of work adjustment teachers in the State of Ohio based on experiences in vocational cooperative programs. These are:

A. *Education:* graduation from approved college or university with specialized training in education in the areas of voca-

tional education, guidance, special education or practical
arts, which special training is to include preparation for
work with academically less able students.

B. *Teaching Experience:* A minimum of two years teaching
experience in vocational education, elementary education,
special education, or two years experience as a guidance
counselor or other comparable activity.

C. *Occupational Experience:* A minimum of twelve months
employment experience in one or more occupations outside of public education.

D. *Personal Qualifications:* The individual shall have a sincere
interest and desire to work with the social academically
handicapped dropout prone youth.

A full unit under our foundation program is approved when
there is a minimum of fifteen students enrolled per work adjustment teacher-coordinator. Maximum enrollment was originally
planned at 30, but the federal requirements for participating in the
five-state experimental program sets a maximum of 20 students per
teacher-coordinator. When a total unit of 15 or more is organized,
the group is divided into two parts so that the teacher has 15 or
less in class at one time. This group of students requires more attention than the normal group of students and, if progress is to be
made with them, individual attention must be provided.

Our experiences with disadvantaged youth would lead us to
believe that successful educational programming for such youth
will have to be coordinated with other services for them. We believe, for example, that vocational rehabilitation, instead of being
a program available only to dropouts and adults, needs to become
an integral part of the educational programming, so that youth who
have physical, mental or social problems beyond the reach of the
educationally trained person may receive such remedial services as
a means of continuing him in school, rather than waiting until he
drops out of school. Experiences also indicates that reading laboratories and related remedial education centers within the school can
be used effectively for youth who may be motivated for the first
time toward reading by giving them the advantage of modern
technology and by placing them in a no-threat situation in which

they are not graded for their achievements in the basic skills important to all people.

Vocational Guidance Implications

I believe this program of occupational work adjustment has significant implications for vocational guidance. It enables the young person to find himself in a success situation in which his efforts are respected. The program should make a great contribution to the ability of the young person to make better vocational choices and better adjustment to the rest of his educational career than if he either continued in school with a self-concept of failure or dropped out of school with the knowledge that he was a reject of the system.

The suggested program is not a vocational training program. Rather, it provides some of the concepts of work evaluation present in vocational rehabilitation services. The required work period in the program can be a changing type of experience. The student might start out on a job in school, build his own self-confidence, and improve his habits of work, then move to a type of employment within the community in which he would gain additional confidence in his ability to compete in our society. The observation of the work experiences by the coordinator can give him a basis to evaluate the potential of the student on something other than his failures in the academic system. A strong desire to achieve and success experiences may overcome some of the differences in ability that the dropout-prone youth may have.

We should never forget that many of the people who can make the greatest contributions to the growth and improvement in our technological society may not be able or willing to participate in the discipline-oriented learning processes presently at the center of our school system. Edison, for example, would not adjust to the school system of his day because his approach to learning was far more in the concrete experiences related to doing than those abstract experiences of reading. Other people who have made a great contribution to our way of life and economy have exhibited the same tendencies as Edison. Such people as Ford, Chrysler, and

Firestone made great contributions without the support of the college preparatory academic background. We should always be watching for the person who isn't interested in being well-rounded, rather has some special fulfillment or realization that is his alone to pursue.

In our frenzy to make everyone the same as everyone else we may be attempting to teach the ducks to run a footrace and the rabbits to swim. The system of vocational guidance and vocational education identified here would maximize the opportunity to adjust the educational program to the individual rather than the individual to the educational program. The experience-centered nature of the program would appeal even to the youth with special abilities and the emphasis upon laboratory periods and community involvement would provide an opportunity for constructive activities.

The services of the guidance counselor can be important throughout the period of time that students are enrolled in the occupational work adjustment program. There could be complete flexibility in terms of mobility of youth in and out of the program. During the school year youth in the regular school program who become disillusioned with their educational progress should have a contact with the guidance counselor, then with the teacher-coordinator of the Work Adjustment program to determine if he can benefit by enrollment in the program. The formal beginning and ending of the school have been artificial barriers to the move-ment of students between educational programs. Just as students should be allowed to move into the work adjustment program dur-ing the school year, youth who find themselves and change their goals while enrolled in the program should be permitted to change their educational curriculum any time during the school year in order to adjust to the program which best fits them. The guidance counselor can be the coordinating agent between the youth in the work adjustment program and the rest of the school program.

While the guidance counselor is not at the core of the pro-gram, it is obvious that he is an important unit in the effort if the program is to be more than a baby-sitting operation to keep troubled students quiet.

I would strongly suggest that the schools move away from their worship of the Carnegie unit which has outlived its purpose

CHARACTERISTICS OF
POTENTIAL SCHOOL DROPOUTS (MARCH 1967)

FACTOR	VULNERABLE TO DROPPING OUT
1. Age	Old for grade group (over 2 years)
2. Physical Size	Small for age group
	Large for age group
3. Health	Frequently ill
	Easily fatigued
4. Participating in School Activities	None
5. Participation in Out-Of School Activities	None
6. Grade Retardation	One year or more retarded
7. Father's Occupation	Unskilled
	Semiskilled
8. Educational Level Achieved by:	
Father	Grade 7 or below
Mother	Grade 7 or below
9. Number of Children in Family	Five or more
10. School-to-school Transfers	Pattern of "jumping from school to school"
11. Attendance	Chronic absenteeism (20 days or more a year)
12. Learning Rate	Below 90 I.Q.
13. Ability to Read	Two years or more below grade level
14. School Marks	Predominantly below "C"
15. Reaction to School Controls	Resents controls
16. Acceptance by Pupils	Not liked
17. Parental Attitude toward Graduation	Negative
	Vacillating
18. Pupil's Interest in School Work	Little or none
19. General Adjustment	Fair or poor

as a means of assuring entrance into the university. The whole impact of this Occupational Work Adjustment program should be motivation for further education, since the programs do not directly train youth for jobs in the economy. The goal should be to motivate them into goal-centered educational programs at grades 11 and 12.

For most of the youth it will be enrollment in a vocational program to prepare for employment immediately upon graduation, but for a few it may be enrollment in a pre-professional program pointing on to college.

I would emphasize again that not all youth who refuse to adjust to the existing education program are dull and unable to achieve. Our brief experiences with this program and with similar work-oriented programs in the State of Ohio would suggest that, given an opportunity to participate in the world of work, the young person may again see himself as a part of an educational program and desire preparation for a beter job than that represented by his initial work experience.

In 1963 a study was completed by our Division of Guidance and Testing and Division of Research covering dropouts from public schools.[1] Dr. Charles Weaver, Supervisor of Guidance Services in that division, summarized the characteristics of potential school dropouts from that report as shown on page 129.

SUMMARY

The characteristics of dropouts are known, can be observed. It remains for the educational system to accept a responsibility of a no-reject concept in which they make an adjustment in the school program to serve these potential school dropouts instead of expecting all young people to adapt to the one concept of education that they have provided for a hundred years. Guidance studies have found youth at the age of 14 or 15 too young to make a reasonable occupation choice, therefore, the vocational education programming has been planned for youth 16 years of age and older. In spite of the research regarding the age of reasonable occupational choice, the experiences of local school systems, particularly in major cities, indicated some new type of programming should be

---

[1] John G. Odgers, Leonard R. Nochman and Russell E. Getson, *Ohio Study of High School Dropouts 1962–63*, Ohio State Dept. of Education, 1964.

provided for youth at age 14. Unless some special type of programming can be provided to dropout prone youth at age 14 and 15, they would not be available at age 16 to enroll in vocational programming relevant to their interests and needs.

Studies of the lower dropout rates in student groups enrolled in vocational programming confirm that concepts of work can be a motivating factor for youth as well as adults. On the basis of evident needs of dropout prone 14 and 15 year olds, I am recommending an occupational work adjustment program now under way in the State of Ohio as a means of providing this group of young people with an educational program that can make them feel socially useful and give them an experience in which they are successful. The program proposed includes a work component, either in the school or in the community, and it is proposed that remuneration for meaningful work is important for the social adjustment of this type of young person. A work adjustment program is proposed as another tool in the system of vocational guidance and vocational education.

Chapter 9   THE POINT OF OCCUPATIONAL CHOICE: AGE 16 AND UP

Vocational Education, A Necessity

As I attend conferences and review guidance literature, counselors talk at length about the area of vocational guidance, but make only passing references with guarded questioning statements on the value or importance of vocational education programs at the high school level. What is the value of a system of vocational guidance if it leads the young person to the point of frustration when he finds there is no opportunity to obtain training in the occupation of his choice?

Our technological society requires training for entrance into most occupations. Industry is not the place to do the basic training in skills and technological knowledge required for entrance into occupations. Yet the literature in vocational guidance shows that professionals tend to stop with the concept of free choice by the student. Can there really be free choice without opportunity to prepare for work?

Guidance counselors seem reluctant to encourage the development of a broad vocational education program in which the youth who have made an occupational choice can receive training as a means of entering into that occupation. They are almost fearful that if a broad vocational program is developed it might somehow restrict some of the students from going on to college at the end of high school. Isn't it rather stupid to fear that students might deviate from an antiquated college preparatory program which has not shown that it has a direct relationship with success in college?

I urge professional guidance counselors to demand of businesses, industries, and the public and vocational educators that the public schools provide a comprehensive educational program. A comprehensive program must include a broad vocational program in which students with varying interests and varying abilities can find a means of preparing for a vocation. To date, the term "comprehensive high school" has been a misnomer, since in practice it was never a truly comprehensive high school, but an academic education center with a sprinkling of co-curricular activities. The presence of some vocational education in a high school does not make that high school comprehensive.

The school district organizations in many states often preclude the ability of the high school in a school district to be comprehensive on the basis of its limited student base and tax base.

Other than major cities, most of the school districts do not have a student base and tax base to provide for a comprehensive vocational education program. The laws of Ohio, therefore, have permitted school districts to join together, forming joint vocational school districts in order to get the student base and tax base necessary for the establishment of a comprehensive vocational education program. Similar practices are followed in other states to provide a basis for a comprehensive vocational education program.

Schools generally offer three course curricula: college preparatory, vocational and general. The vocational is built around the occupational goal of the student. He receives instruction in the skills and technical knowledge necessary for successful entrance into an occupation supplemented by the required high school courses. The college preparatory program normally includes subject-centered instruction in mathematics, science, English, and history as the basic subjects for the four-year high school program. The general program is a hodge-podge of courses taken in practically any relationship so that the student can achieve the necessary 16¾ units credit to graduate from high school, neither prepared to go to college nor prepared to go to work.

We know that no craftsmen can work without tools. How can a system of vocational guidance have any meaning if it does not have available the tool of a broad vocational education program in addition to a college preparatory program and general program?

Youth at the age of 16 are just as different psychologically from those of ages 14 and 15 as the youth differ physiologically at age 12 and 13 from those at ages 10 and 11. We have long recognized the physiological changes in youth but ignore the psychological changes. Ideally, a change in the educational programming, including housing at the seventh grade, is intended to recognize the physiological change, although I do not believe that the present curriculum achieves this. We have refused, moreover, to recognize that young people at age 16 are looking forward to participating in the adult society, and they know that the only way of really entering into that adult society is through work. A man's job is his ticket to adulthood. Until he has that job and is self-supporting, a driver's license or the ability to purchase a glass of beer does not make him a member of the adult society.

One of the modern leaders of educational theory, Robert J. Havighurst, a noted social scientist and educator, identified the needs of youth on a developmental basis. One need was to develop towards independence. Why can't educators recognize this need and see that independence is directly related to the ability of the individual to provide for himself? There is some loose thinking by educators as a whole and guidance counselors in particular that the way to prepare for entrance into our modern technology is to give the students a smattering of everything so they will be flexible as they adjust to changes. They raise the question, "How do we know what jobs will be available in 1980," without any concern for how the young people who will graduate in June, 1970 will earn a living until 1980.

I believe that educational theory and principles of learning indicate that a person who has prepared himself for an occupation

by studying in depth the skills and technical knowledge involved
and who has seen a relationship between theory and practice, including an understanding of the functions of math and principles
of science as they may apply, is more able to adjust to learn a new
occupation than the person who, as he learns only a little bit about
a number of jobs, does not learn enough about any one of them
to have suffered the discipline required to achieve success in an
occupation. I am sure that educators as a whole, and guidance
counselors in particular, are sincere in their interest in youth, but
I believe that their very lack of experiences in terms of the world
of work and a sort of secret belief that those jobs aren't very
important anyway leads them to some very fuzzy thinking regard'
ing vocational educational programs.

Under the Federal Manpower Development and Training
programs, providing training for the unemployed, the unemployed
who got the best jobs, and who stayed employed the longest at the
highest pay, were those who had been given a depth of institutional
vocational training. They didn't study in a general occupational
area, but in identifiable job families such as machine trade, welding, secretarial, practical nursing, drafting and other occupational
areas which have been the backbone of the vocational programming within our state and nation.

The programming under the Manpower Development and
Training Act of 1963 (MDTA) is tied directly to the needs of the
labor market in terms of work opportunity. In comparing the offerings in MDTA programming with the vocational education programming offered by our public schools, we have found almost a
100 percent match in terms of program emphasis. Let's quit talking
about general this and general that, because such generalities are
related to general employment. Educational research tells us that if
the young person doesn't use knowledge he will forget it. For
transfer of learning to take place, most of us need that transfer
pointed out and taught.

Can't we finally accept the concept that experience is a center-
point for all learning, and that experience in learning an occupation through practical applications of the skills of that occupation

can also be a center for teaching what principles of the disciplines that apply to those occupations?

Broad Program Needed

There can be no system of vocational guidance and vocational education unless the vocational education program available has sufficient breadth to enable the youth to enroll in a program relating to their interests and abilities. In the last session of the Ohio Legislature, a law was passed requiring every school to offer an adequate program of vocational education or to join with other school districts to offer an adequate program of vocational education. The law stated that any school district with less than 1,500 in the upper four grades could not plan alone. The State Board of Education, in establishing standards to interpret the word "adequate", has outlined a minimum adequacy of program as 12 different vocational offerings and 20 vocational classes. A vocational offering could be interpreted as auto mechanics, secretarial training, distributive education, production agriculture or any one of a number of occupational classifications. Thus the state standards require that 12 different programs of this type be offered. In reference to the 20 classes, there might, for example, be two classes in auto mechanics counted toward the 20. While Ohio has one of the broadest cooperative education programs in the nation, a maximum of four cooperative programs could be counted within the minimum 12 required programs.

The limitation to four cooperative programs in a minimum scope program was not to indicate that cooperative education is not an important part of the vocational programming, but that the total programming should not depend upon all cooperative positions. Variations in the economy, and the fact that some occupations do not lend themselves well to cooperative experiences, would suggest that when a minimum program is considered, it should include more than cooperative experiences. Our Division of Vocational Education in the State Department of Education has indi-

cated that a minimum program might include the following type of
offerings: Three agricultural programs, three business and office
programs, two distributive education programs, one job training
program relating to home economics, and five trade and industrial
programs.[1]

This tentative listing of a minimum vocational education
program is not a blueprint for all areas served by vocational education. It is used here only as illustration of programs that could be
provided.

A study completed for the State Legislature by Dr. Ralph
Purdy professor at Miami University, Oxford, Ohio in 1966 indicated that a desirable program of vocational education could be
accomplished with an enrollment of 1,100 to 1,200 students in the
vocational programs. This type of enrollment would allow the offering of 28 to 30 different vocational education offerings, accom-
modating the less able through the above average students. The
program at Penta County Joint Vocational School in Ohio enrolls
1,100 and offers the following:

A. Agriculture
   1. Training for non-production agricultural occupations
   2. Vocational horticulture
   3. Advanced farm business management and account-
      ing
   4. Advanced agricultural equipment and mechanics

B. Business Education
   1. High skill steno/entry secretarial 11-12
   2. Account clerk 11-12
   3. Entry business data processor 11-12
   4. Office machines operator 11-12
   5. Cooperative office education (12th only)
   6. Office reproduction specialist 11-12
   7. Intensive horizontal business office education (12th
      only)

---

[1] Byrl R. Shoemaker, "A Position Paper on Vocational Education in the Public Schools," Ohio State Dept. of Education, Division of Vocational Education
(unpublished).

C. Distributive Education
   1. Retail selling, buying and pricing of merchandising and personnel management

D. Home Economics
   1. Child care assistant
   2. Child care worker
   3. Homemaker's assistant
   4. Dietary aid

E. Trade and Industrial Education
   1. Machine trades
   2. Auto mechanics
   3. Auto body repair
   4. Cosmetology
   5. Drafting
   6. Electrical construction
   7. Commercial art
   8. Carpentry
   9. Dental assistant
   10. Medical laboratory assistant
   11. Industrial electronics
   12. Welding and sheet metal
   13. Commercial foods
   14. Printing

F. Occupational Work Experience Program

The state standards projected in compliance with the law passed by the state legislature is then indeed *minimum*. But by its bold action, despite massive efforts by a few small inadequate districts to restrict the standards, the State Board of Education in Ohio has made educational history in requiring the educational system to recognize its responsibility for the education of all youth.

Many people are confused about the differences between vocational and technical education. I believe that these two areas of education are closely related, but I would suggest two definitions which may be helpful in identifying these two areas of education which prepare people for jobs.

Technical Education is an area of education more practical than the professional and more theoretical than that of the craftsman. It is a new area of post high school education—not a watering down of professional education and not an upward extension of trade or vocational education. It is a level of education to prepare for new *levels* of employment in business, industry, agriculture, distribution, health, and the social sciences concerned with functions of design, development, testing, and supervision. It is a program to prepare people to work as para-professionals in a team relationship with a professional in that occupation.

Technical education is a level of education that is growing in keeping with our technological revolution. Its growth is based on the concept of the increasing requirements and changes in assignments in the professional field and on the shrinking number of professional people per thousand of population. This level of education is planned to prepare para-professional people in 2-year post high school programs to work in a team relationship with professional people in engineering, business, agriculture, distribution, health, social science, and public service.

The primary purpose of *vocational education* is to equip persons for useful employment. The program is designed to serve the needs of people in two distinct groups: first, adults who have entered the world of work; and second, youth and adults who are preparing to enter occupations in agriculture, business, homemaking, distribution, trade, technical, and industrial fields requiring less than a college degree. Vocational education is concerned with the preparation of people for construction, maintenance, repair, and servicing occupations.

Vocational education contributes to the general education needs of youth, such as citizenship, respect for others, and acceptance of responsibilities; but it makes its unique contribution in the field of preparation for work.

Now, how are these definitions related to employment areas and what are the relationships? The five examples that follow are representative of team relationships among various types of occupational areas:

Industrial Area
    Professional —Mechanical engineer
    Technical   —Tool and die designer
    Skilled   —Tool and die maker
    Semiskilled —Drill Press operator

Business Area
    Professional —Accountant (college graduate)
    Technical   —Business data computer programmer
    Skilled   —Unit record operator
    Semiskilled —Clerk

Agriculture Area
    Professional —Agriculture engineer
    Technical   —Agriculture equipment distributor
    Skilled   —Agriculture equipment repair
    Semiskilled —Agriculture equipment delivery

Health Area
    Professional —Dentist
    Technical   —Dental hygienist
    Skilled   —Dental assistant
    Semiskilled —Dental office clerk

Social Science Area
    Professional —Lawyer
    Technical   —Tax technician
    Skilled   —Stenographer
    Semiskilled —File clerk

The needs of the people for jobs and need of jobs for people have encouraged a broad expansion of vocational and technical education in our state. It isn't enough to have vocational education in name only, the vocational programs must be of such depth as to truly prepare the young people for entrance as advanced learners in the occupation of their choice. Most of the vocational programs in the State of Ohio involve three-fourths of the student's day during the last two years of his occupational career. The student's choice of an occupation becomes the core around which the skills related to that occupation are taught in sufficient depth for employment either through instruction in a school laboratory with facilities and equipment similar to those found in industry and business or through a cooperative experience on the job. In addition to the instruction in the skills of an occupation, the functions of mathematics and the principles of science are taught in relationship to that occupation as a required part of that program. The principles of learning tell us that people learn when they see a meaning for what they are learning and that they learn by doing. The type of program described above provides a student the opportunity to do and to put into practice the mathematics and science important to that occupation. In any licensed occupation, such as cosmetology, students completing programs in our public schools take the license examination upon completion of their program the same as students from any other cosmetology school.

I believe that we must maintain a continuing program of post-high school vocational and technical education services to assist individuals to train for their first job when they have missed such training in high school or desire to prepare for a technical occupation requiring an associate degree, to retrain for another job when they find themselves out of employment, or to upgrade themselves by study at vocational centers while they are employed as full time workers.

Guidance Services

When students are ready to choose an occupation or occupation cluster, guidance counselors should be able to help them evaluate their interests, abilities and chances for success. Many guidance counselors have great qualms about encouraging a young person to make an occupational choice at age 16, even though such a choice is tentative and can be changed at a later date. On the other hand, they seem to have absolutely no qualms about encouraging a young person to follow a college preparatory curriculum, even though only 14 out of every 100 who start first grade will complete a college education.[2]

Vocational programs prepare youth for employment without denying them an opportunity to change their minds regarding college. Annually about 10 percent of our graduates from our vocational programs change their goals and go on to college. Studies indicate that if they were good students in vocational education and have the ability to read, write and think, they can succeed in their college careers. The person who is really handicapped upon completion of high school education is the one who has made no choice. For most young people, however, the high school program is their last opportunity for a full-time educational offering. It is highly critical, therefore, that students have adequate counseling in choosing their vocational interest.

Interest and aptitude tests can be of service to the student. Ohio's Division of Guidance and Testing has developed the Ohio Vocational Interest Survey (OVIS) for counselors to use. The General Aptitude Test Battery (GATB), available from all state employment services offices in the nation, is probably the most comprehensive aptitude test on the market. Counselors are trained by the employment services in the administration of the GATB. Such tests are not, however, a substitute for experience. They supplement experience and perhaps become more meaningful when they can be related to actual work.

As important as testing may be, a vocational guidance system dependent solely on occupational information, interest testing and aptitude testing is doomed to failure.

A study conducted in 1965 by Coleman[**] and others found that when a group of twelfth grade boys were asked to indicate the type of job in which they expected to enter when they finished their education, more than half of these indicated they expected to occupy professional and managerial positions.

---

[2] Figures provided by the Ohio State Department of Education and Board of Regents.

[**] James S. Coleman and others, *Equality of Educational Opportunity,* U.S. Department of Health, Education, and Welfare, Office of Education, (OE-38001) (Washington: U.S. Government Printing Office, 1966).

In tests administered to over 200,000 Ohio youth through our Division of Guidance and Testing, only 3 to 4 percent in any individual community or on a statewide basis will indicate "no choice" of an occupational goal. Further probing, however, shows that many have unrealistic occupational goals in terms of their abilities and the employment opportunities within the economy. The paper-pencil and information approach to occupational choice fails. *I believe that the only answer is the development of a vocational guidance system based upon experience and centered in the curriculum.*

Placement and Follow-up

Guidance counselors have failed to accept a responsibility for placement and follow-up services for graduates. Guidance counselors existing in the schools today can point to the added work placed on them by the administration which is not work of guidance and counseling, but it has been my observation that misuse is made of people when they themselves do not have meaningful activities making a major contribution to the educational program in a manner that is recognized by the school administration. I would suggest to those guidance counselors who believe that they are misused by the school administrators that such misuse may be more a fault of their own than that of the administration, that such activities may be a crutch used by the counselors to justify their position in the school, and that this practice will change only when the counselors can point to significant important activities that they must carry out on the basis of student needs, not goals of the profession.

I question how many counselors are thoroughly familiar with the industries and businesses located in their labor market area. Generalized knowledge about jobs and employment trends is no substitute for relationships with existing industries which can provide a more meaningful approach to jobs and job opportunities than all the labor market data collected on nationwide trends. Industries and businesses have proven again and again their interest in cooperating with the schools. The counselors who have been school centered can hardly understand that most of the larger industries and businesses of today have gained a social consciousness in relationship to their responsibilities for disadvantaged youth and adults as well as their profit motive so necessary to survival.

I do not propose that our public schools take over the responsibilities of the State Employment Service, since the responsibilities of that organization represent a continuing service for placement for adults as they change jobs during the work career. I am suggesting, however, that a special service of placement and follow-up is a logical function of the public education system since the graduates are their product. For years the vocational education programs within the public schools of our nation have placed graduates in jobs or further education and annually must report on this effort to our State Division of Vocational Education. This placement and follow-up service of our Division of Vocational Education has been a significant factor in keeping programs in vocational education related to the needs of people and the needs of industry and business. Recent federal laws in the area of vocational education require improved procedures of placement and follow-up to help in guiding the further development of the vocational programs. Possibly, vocational guidance counselors can and should be prepared to assume a responsibility toward placement and follow-up of all high school youth, including those from the college preparatory program and those who drop out before graduation.

The legislative arm of our government is indicating that our educational system must be responsible for either placing young persons in a job upon completion of, or leaving high school, or enrolling them in additional educational programs after graduation. This is a significant change from the concept of a school system which says, "it's our responsibility to shovel knowledge to students like we would coal to a furnace, and if they don't want it they should get out of the system."

Public education does not have the right to throw its rejects into the ranks of the unemployed and underemployed in our community. It must be responsible for satisfactory adjustment of their product, the youth of our nation, to the society in which they live. The area of placement and follow-up is a rare opportunity for the vocational guidance counselor as an immediate service to youth and a means of re-evaluating and reorganizing the system through the follow-up data. The system must adapt to the needs of youth, not youth to the system.

SUMMARY

A system of vocational guidance is sterile unless the young person can enroll in a program which will prepare him for entrance into employment related to his occupational choice. Since high school is the last opportunity for most young people to participate in a full-time educational program, it is unthinkable that we would suggest that all vocational education be held until the post-high school period. Experience shows that an adequate program of vocational education retains youth in high school longer. Vocational programs are a greater stimulus for youth to grow toward adulthood than the so-called general programs.

A broad program of vocational education is essential if youth have been led to a point of significant occupational choice by the age of 16. Some vocational education is not enough. A comprehensive educational program must include a comprehensive vocational program which has within it a broad range of offerings. It must be able to consider the varying interests and ability levels of the youth and the employment opportunities available within the local labor market.

While interest tests and aptitude tests are an important tool of the vocational guidance counselor, such tests, even when used with occupational information, represent an unworkable approach to vocational guidance. These tools can be meaningful only if the educational system has included a system of vocational guidance based upon experience—experience which develops positive attitudes toward work, experience which provides an understanding of the world of work. The system should provide each youth with an opportunity to explore occupations in terms of his interests and abilities; it should help youth to focus all of these experiences into an occupational choice.

No young person can be truly independent of his parents or others unless he is able to earn his own way. Existence on welfare is not independence. Let me speak for young people. They do not want to be kept busy by a program established by the state, local or federal government. They do not want doles and handouts which destroy their manhood, their self-respect and which relegate them to second-class citizens. They want an opportunity for a job which will pay them a living wage.

We will either provide the youth with an opportunity for training for a job and an opportunity to work following such training, or we will fight them in the streets. My efforts as Governor of the State of Ohio and efforts in any future public position I might hold will be to provide the youth with opportunity for choice, with training for work and with an opportunity for work within our economy after they complete training, whether this training is at the high school, post-high school or collegiate level. Only radical changes in our educational system can save us from a welfare society. A system of vocational guidance and vocational education must be at the core of those changes.

Chapter 10   CHANCE FOR CHANGE

Challenge and Opportunity

The total educational system within our nation is being measured and found wanting. The massive social and economic problems within our nation cry out for solutions, not for commiseration. These problems must be solved or our nation will become a welfare state with a fair sharing of less and less goods and services. Our educational system will either change and become a positive force in solving the problems besetting our nation, or another type of institution will be developed from the federal level which will direct its attention to these problems. In blunt language, either the educational systems of our state and nation will accept their social and economic responsibilities, or we will see the development of a federal system of education, initially identified as concerned with Manpower training.

My whole-hearted support is for change and improvement in our existing educational system. I fear and distrust any national system of education under whatever guise that would find a way to the minds of men. It has been my experience that direct federal ventures into the area of education have been massively expensive, woefully ineffective and likely to be used as a means of building a political power structure.

There must be a rallying point around which the public educational system can draw the support of Congress, state legislatures, the public, industry, business, parents and students. The system of vocational guidance and vocational education proposed in this book can be such a rallying point for the massive changes needed in our educational system. I believe that any massive new investments in the educational system at state and federal levels will come only if the administrators and legislators at those levels believe that our public educational system can make a significant contribution to the problems of our day. I do not believe that they are interested in supporting at a higher funding level an educational system which accepts no responsibility for its product and which has concerned itself at the high school with only a small percentage of the youth who will be provided a means of earning a living through vocational preparation at colleges and universities. If the educational system does accept the challenge for change and a major responsibility for solving the social and economic problems that we face, then that system has a right to require that it be provided with funds necessary to implement such changes.

When we read about investments in the Job Corps averaging $9,000 to $12,000 per enrollee, when we read about investments in federal Manpower programs in short-term on-the-job training programs under the National Alliance for Businessmen costing $3,000 to $4,000 per person, when we realize that a delinquent person maintained in one of our state institutions costs us $4,000 to $5,000 per year, we can see that it will be necessary to make investments in education beyond the bare 30-pupils-per-teacher type of investments that we make at the present time. We must find ways to involve supporting services such as physical, mental and social rehabilitation, remedial education, and educational and personal counseling. The added investments can be justified on the basis that we either make the person whole and productive in our economy or we subsidize him and his family throughout their lifetimes.

The system of vocational guidance and vocational education suggested in this book, if established at the core of the curriculum in the elementary and senior high school, could serve not only as the basis for added services to all youth, but as a basis for revitalizing the whole curriculum. As the social and economic concerns of the system of vocational guidance and vocational education change the attitudes of the teachers and administrators, the content and organization of the total educational program will in turn be changed. A massive cooperative effort by professionals in vocational education and guidance may well be a starting point or a rallying point for the initiation of a system of vocational guidance and vocational education. No major changes will be made in the public education system, however, unless the community and political resources are willing to encourage and fund such changes in the system. Voters in our state and in the nation have clearly indicated that they are disillusioned with the quality of our educational system and they are no longer willing to fund the status quo. Perhaps I am suggesting that final decisions on changes in the educational system do not rest with the professional people in education, but with the various publics that fund the educational system and are the recipients of the services of that system. Since tax funds are at the heart of the funding of the educational system, we cannot ignore the fact that the people and the political process of our republic eventually determine the function that the educational system is to serve.

Decisions

Our present educational system probably is tolerated because of the massive good will that it built up several decades past when an education other than reading, writing and arithmetic may not have been very important except to those who went on to college. It is very possible now, however, that the mass of disillusioned people for whom the present educational program has not been relevant may look to another agency of government to serve their needs. At the vocational level a bill has been introduced into Congress which would provide to the Department of Labor $2 billion to be used for remedial programs for people who are out of school and not participating in the labor market. Part of that legislation would let the Department of Labor provide services of a work-experience nature to youth as far down as the ninth grade.

Education represents a way to the minds of men. The present state and local control of our educational system prevents any organization, group or individual at the national level from getting control of the minds of our youth. Our very freedom depends upon the maintenance of a free educational system. This system must not be perverted by the insidious growth of a national system of education under the guise of manpower training.

The massive changes that I have suggested involve the development of a system of vocational guidance and vocational education that will not only provide for the development of vocational orientation, exploration and training programs, but will serve as a catalyst for the redirection of the present curriculum. I do not suggest the destruction or replacement of the existing educational system, but a massive revision of that system. I do not propose the employment of a whole new cadre of teachers, but a conversion of the existing teachers for the K-6 grades' World of Work program, 7-8 grades' career orientation program and the 9-10 grades' career exploration program. Additional guidance counselors will be needed for coordination and leadership efforts in these programs and additional vocational personnel needed for the expanded vocational programs at grades 11 and 12, or age 16 and older.

The system that I propose would enable all youth in the elementary school to become aware of the world of work, to respect the work of all people and to respect the people themselves, and to look toward work as fulfilling to themselves and a responsibility to the society in which they will live.

The system would provide all youth at ages 12 and 13 with an opportunity to learn about the various types of jobs, including professions, which make up the world of work in a technological age, and the economic facts concerning the productive and service segments of that society. At this age level they would be encouraged to not only examine the world of work, but to see themselves as a part of that world of work. Self-analysis would be encouraged within the framework that all work is honorable and important.

The system would provide all youth at ages 14 and 15, or grades 9 and 10, with the opportunity to explore the future open to them in various jobs, professions or job families, the nature of the work involved, and the qualifications necessary for success. The career exploration program would be based upon the choices of the individual student. The scope of the exploration program should be such as to include the social and economic sectors of the community. What could be more important at these age levels than a chance to sample and examine areas of work in which to invest their future? Even a humble occupation approached on the basis of choice and commitment can be a career in terms of the self-esteem of the individual and his contribution to society. For this age level there would be a special work adjustment program for dropout-prone youth.

The system would provide a chance for choice of vocational or pre-professional education at ages 16 and above, or grades 11 and 12. For the concept of choice to be most meaningful there must be a comprehensive vocational education program with twenty-five or more different vocational education offerings and a comprehensive pre-professional program built around the broad professional areas. The program for this age level would provide goal-centered education.

At the core of each of the segments of the system would be the concept of experience-based and curriculum-centered educational programming.

The massive changes that I am suggesting in the curriculum from kindergarten through grade 12 certainly will require the backing of more than one person or one group. Since I believe sincerely that many individuals and groups must join in this effort, I want to speak first to the most concerned persons, to parents.

To the Parent

I realize that there is no person in the world more interested in a boy or girl than the parent. You want your sons and daughters to have a better opportunity in life than you had, so you push your children towards occupations which you believe will achieve this goal. Isn't it possible, however, that parental concerns for the welfare of your young person gets confused with your status concerns for his place in society? Some parents unwittingly relive their lives through their children and create problems for the young people rather than help them find solutions.

Research in vocational guidance suggests that the parents are the most important factor in the occupational choice or educational goals established by the youth. It seems, therefore, that the attitude and judgements of parents are a major factor in the development of any changes in the public education system.

Many, maybe most parents, want their children to go to college so "they won't have to work like I do." This massive push towards college goals on the part of parents exists even in the lower social economic scale, since high aspirations are not limited to any one economic group. However, present figures indicate that only about 14 of every 100 youth starting the first grade will finish college, and that in 1970 only 11 to 12 percent of our population will be employed in professions. These facts suggest that youth should be exposed to a broad orientation to the job opportunities in our society. They should especially become aware of the many skilled and technical occupations not requiring enrollment in a university. You, as parents, must become more realistic and encourage the public schools to do the type of programming to provide your son or daughter the chance for choice and the chance for training. The alternative for them is a lifetime of menial jobs interrupted by long stretches of unemployment.

How can you help? You can help by encouraging your school system to initiate a system of vocational guidance in the elementary, junior high school and high school years, and a comprehensive program of vocational education leading to employment upon graduation. Attend and participate in your parent-teacher organizations. Write to your school superintendent that you want more guidance and vocational education for your children. Write to your congressman and your state legislators encouraging their commitments to legislation which will develop a broad system of vocational guidance and vocational education in our public schools. Indicate that you know the changes will cost more money now, but will be a savings in the long run. Indicate your willingness to support those increased costs.

To School Board Members

You represent the liaison between the public and the professional educators. No major educational changes are possible within your school or within your state as a whole unless you, as a member of a local or state board of education, permit or encourage such changes in the school program. An addition to your school system of a program of vocational guidance and vocational education represents a major curricular change. The cost for the vocational guidance part of the program may not be as massive as you would believe since the proposed program would utilize many of the existing resources through a reorganization of those resources rather than through the establishment of new and competing programs in the curriculum.

You may find it necessary, however, to encourage your school district to join with other neighboring districts in order to bring together the student base and tax base necessary for a broad program of vocational education. The vocational end of the proposal would cost more, but experiences in our state would suggest that the operational cost of a depth program of vocational education would be only $320 more per year per student than for the general high school program. If you compare this cost to cost of welfare or the cost of any of the federal manpower programs, you can find that such an expenditure is more of an investment than it is a cost.

The professional educators whom you employ can and should be responsible for the development and the implementation of the programs that I suggest. You as a board member, however, must be willing to be a part of the procedure for interpreting these changes to the community. You must accept a leadership role in this regard and not place the total responsibility for educational change upon the educational administrators that you employ. Do you really know about the educational needs of all youth or are you affected by the affluent parents who want you to make sure that their son or daughter can enter Harvard? Do you truly represent all parents in the community as you sit on the school board? Do you represent the parents of the students who have been failed by the system as well as those who graduate at the head of their class? Have you encouraged the size of an educational district which will permit the establishment of a comprehensive program of vocational education or have you insisted upon maintaining a small school district fiscally uneconomical and educationally unfeasible?

Education in our nation has had a history of local control through lay boards of education. A system of local control is now on trial by a nation beset by problems that cry out for solution. Your commitment must take into account the needs of all of the youth.

To Leaders in Industry and Business

I am greatly encouraged by the attitudes of leaders in industry and business as they accept a social responsibility for maintaining a viable business and profit economy.

I also realize, however, that at times there is a temptation to reach for the educational dollar offered by a federal government overtly expressing the wish to serve the disadvantaged youth and adult. I would point up to you, however, that the tremendous cost of serving youth and adults through the present Manpower training programs makes impossible provisions for such services to any more than a few of the people who have such needs. I would ask you to realize that the excessive educational costs of the Manpower programs present no solution to the social and economic problems and only suggest higher and higher investments in remedial programs since they offer no solutions. I would suggest that you examine carefully this Trojan Horse offered by a Department of Labor anxious and eager to become a national education agency. In your haste to accept the $3,000 per trainee made available under the National Alliance for Businessmen, I believe that you should ask yourself if your function is one of education or one of production. Do you really have the expertise to do more than polish the individual and to shove him into an unskilled job even though that job may be paying a good wage?

What are the political implications if we eventually arrive at a Department of Labor which has control of Manpower training and control of the employment service? And make no mistake about it, our state employment services are totally dependent upon the Department of Labor for funding. I see no evidence which indicates that the training in industry has either been as effective as institutional training under a public education system or as economical in terms of cost.

Experiences in our state indicate that you are very willing to support the expansion of programs of vocational education. You realize that the future of industry rests with the education of our youth and that the jobs that you have to offer today require skills and technical knowledge. You have proven to be an effective force in the building of vocational education programs within our state and I would now enlist your support in encouraging both the reorganization of our educational system in the state to provide for effective and economical school district units, and the reorganization of the curriculum to involve a system of vocational guidance and vocational education.

Your industries and businesses under such a system would become an extension of the school program at the elementary school level. You would be asked to talk to the students to motivate them to want to work at some part of the work of the world. You would be asked to let them visit your plant to gain a respect for all work. At the junior high school level, youth would visit your industry or business to gain an understanding of the technological society in which we live and the broad number of occupations present in those industries and businesses ranging from the unskilled to the professional. You would be involved in the exploration program and work adjustment program for 14 and 15 year olds as they evaluate their interests and abilities in terms of an occupational choice. You would be involved in the vocational programming for young people 16 years and above in terms of the scope and content of the vocational programs and the participation of students working in your industries and businesses on cooperative type programs under school supervision and in cooperation with study in-school.

Yes, the changes needed in our school system ask more than your tacit support. The changes that I propose will require your active involvement.

To Labor Leaders

No organization or group in our nation has been more concerned with the educational process than organized labor. You pioneered in the area of child labor legislation to free the youth from oppressive employment so they could obtain an education.

Through the efforts of Samuel Gompers and other leaders of his day, you made a major contribution to the development of vocational education in this nation. In our effort to protect youth from the dangers of oppressive and dangerous employment, however, we have denied youth the work experiences at a very critical age in their lives when such experiences can mean much to them. The whole direction of my program suggestions for a system of vocational guidance and vocational education are pointed toward experiences for career choice and vocational education for employment.

The changes that I propose cannot be implemented in a school system without the constructive effort of organized labor. Organized labor has a stake in the education of all youth to respect work, in the orientation of all youth to a technical society, in the process of exploration by each person for occupational choice and in the vocational programs planned to help youth prepare to enter the occupation of their choice.

You, along with the other segments of our society, have joined in a commitment to eradicate poverty—a program which cannot accept unemployment for any significant part of the social structure. The system proposed in this book is planned to provide every youth the knowledge and skills needed to either go to work upon graduation from high school or to enter further education. Furthermore, the program is designed so that a young person is not ruled out of chances for further education if he changes his mind. Your major responsibility would be to assist in making a place for all the graduates who are ready to enter employment. Your attitudes towards them can prove them a success or make them a failure.

To Federal Government Policy-makers

The legislation before you could be oversimplified to indicate that you had a choice between the continuation of the profits motive in our economy or the movement toward a welfare state. The recent report of the President's Commission on Income Maintenance Programs entitled "Poverty Amid Plenty —The American Paradox" completely ignores the public education system as a basis for vocational guidance and vocational training. If the education system were doing its job, we could reduce the amount of remedial education and remedial job training that has proven so costly under the Manpower Development and Training programs. At no point in the document is a public education system mentioned as a force that can be used for solutions. Instead, the document directs itself to an ever-expanding investment in remedial programs even though the report recognizes that the costs of such programs would permit service to no more than a small percentage of those needing such services.

You are being asked to consider a comprehensive manpower training bill which would place the responsibility for a broad educational program into the hands of the Department of Labor. While the bill suggests that the programs would be operated from the state level, the state would be permitted to operate them only as the programs satisfy the Department of Labor. If we are going to give the Department of Labor jurisdiction over the vocational education programs which they would rename "Manpower Program," then we should transfer the Department of Education from the Department of Health, Education, and Welfare to the Department of Labor.

Members of Congress knowledgeable about the services of the educational program in their local communities have supported legislation which provides funds for the strengthening of educational programs in the public schools of our nation, including the vocational education services. Federal funds provided to the states by the federal government for vocational education have been matched two or three to one by state and local monies. Over 7 million youth and adults were served by the vocational and technical programs in our public schools during the 1969 fiscal year with a federal investment of approximately 250 million dollars. The federal budget for this year provided 420 million dollars to the Department of Labor to provide some type of on-the-job training for 140,000 people under the National Alliance for Businessmen's Program. Does this make economic sense?

The Vocational Education Amendments of 1968 have encouraged our states to develop within our public school system a total system of vocational guidance and vocational education as described in this book. Under the Vocational Education Amendments of 1968, P.L. 88-210, Congress authorized the appropriation of approximately $800 million for vocational and technical education. Congress authorized $800 million under the Amendments but at the time this book is being written, Congress is having great difficulty in making more money available than was available prior to the passage of the Act. Congress seems to be willing but needs the support of national policy.

Federal funds are needed to stimulate the program of vocational guidance and vocational education that I have described. The vehicle for these investments can be the federal-state-local relationship established in vocational education. I would plead with the federal government policy makers to strengthen this federal-state-local relationship and to provide funds in keeping with the appropriations authorized under the Vocational Education Amendments of 1968.

I would encourage federal government policy makers to fund programs which provide solutions rather than remedial programs which take only a few from the pool of the unemployed while our public schools pour hundreds of thousands into the pool annually.

To State Legislators and Governors

The responsibility for education does not rest with the educator, but with the people to whom they're responsible. Education is a responsibility of the state. All states have chosen to share this responsibility with state and local boards of education. It remains the responsibility of the state legislature and state administration, however, to determine whether the educational system is indeed accepting the responsibilities assigned to that system and to assist that system to carry out its assigned responsibilities through the state funds provided to the educational programs in the local communities.

The nature of the economic problems facing our school system and the competition for the tax dollar would suggest that improvements in our educational system may depend upon expanded state and federal funds and the wise use of such funds. Allocations to local schools should be made on the basis of purposes for which it is to be used and a commitment of the schools to initiate the program. The mere inclusion of an additional amount of money in any foundation program does not guarantee the initiation of any programs. Money provided beyond a basic foundation allowance should be assigned on a categorical aid basis to school districts or programs which they agree to implement in accordance with standards developed by the state department of education.

In most states, programs of vocational education are encouraged through the allocation of state and/or federal funds specifically for those programs. It cannot be considered encouragement, however, if the additional assistance provided for vocational programs is so limited as to limit the development of a total program of vocational education within the state. Vocational education costs more, but vocational education is an investment towards solutions to a social and economic problem.

Direct state and federal investment also may be necessary in the proposed system of vocational guidance in grades kindergarten thru 10 in order to encourage the implementation of this program throughout all schools in the state. No new investment should cover the total cost of the program suggested. Rather, the existing educational sources should be converted to the new programming and financing provided for the extra program costs and the costs of transition. A rough estimate is that the vocational guidance system in grades K through 10 might be implemented at an annual cost of $20 to $25 per student.

More money must be invested in our educational system if we expect it to solve our social and economic problems. The mere addition of money, however, will not guarantee any changes. As distasteful as it may seem to many people, categorical aid patterns will be necessary at both the state and national levels if we are to implement the changes necessary in the public education system. The investments of a reasonable amount of money in vocational guidance and vocational education systems could bring about massive changes in the total educational system. The proposed curriculum would not only affect student attitudes and experiences, but it would affect teacher attitudes as well. Research of the past supports change; projections for the future support change; social and economic problems faced today support change. Let's utilize our most important source for solutions of social and economic problems—the public education system.

Action Necessary

I have directed special statements to vocational guidance counselors, vocational educators, school administrators or teachers. Essentially the whole thrust of the book is toward this group of people who must take the initiative and leadership if the suggestions made here are to be anything other than idle words. I have been critical of the present system of guidance, but this does not imply criticisms of individual counselors as they go about their daily tasks of providing services within the existing system. I have become acquainted with the people in vocational education and guidance perhaps better than I have in any of the other facets of the school program because of their drive and desire to make changes in that educational system to better serve both youth and adults. I know of no more committed group of people in the field of education than those in vocational education and in guidance nor a group more ready and able to attempt to make changes in the system.

In developing a system of vocational education and guidance, guidance counselors have nothing to lose but their frustrations. My proposal insists that the program of vocational guidance be curriculum-centered, that the success of the system will be based upon the acceptance of the systems by the teacher and school administrators. This puts the teacher in the curriculum at the heart of the vocational guidance system but still leaves an important place for the trained vocational guidance counselor to make his contribution. The ultimate goal of the system should be to encourage the young people to want to "do something" rather than "be somebody." The end product of the system of vocational guidance and vocational education should be a worker competent in whatever task he chooses, aware of his social and civic responsibilities, and confident of his ability to face the future.